ALSO BY CAROL CASSELL:

Straight from the Heart: How to Talk to Your
Teenagers About Love and Sex

SWEPT AWAY

WHY WOMEN CONFUSE LOVE AND SEX

Carol Cassell, Ph.D.

A FIRESIDE BOOK PUBLISHED BY SIMON & SCHUSTER INC.
NEW YORK   LONDON   TORONTO   SYDNEY   TOKYO

Fireside
Simon & Schuster Building
Rockefeller Center
1230 Avenue of the Americas
New York, New York 10020

First Fireside Edition, 1989
FIRESIDE and colophon are registered trademarks of
Simon & Schuster Inc.
Designed by Karolina Harris
Manufactured in the United States of America
1   3   5   7   9   10   8   6   4   2
1   3   5   7   9   10   8   6   4   2   Pbk.

Library of Congress Cataloging in Publication Data
Cassell, Carol
Swept away: why women fear their own sexuality/Carol Cassell. —
1st Fireside ed.
p.   cm.
Bibliography: p.
1. Women—United States—Sexual behavior.   2. Women—United
States—Psychology.   I. Title.
HQ29.C39   1989
306.7'088042—dc19   89-5937
CIP
ISBN 0-671-45238-X
ISBN 0-671-68183-4 Pbk.

The author gratefully acknowledges permission from the following
sources to quote material in the text:

"Hers" by Barbara Lazear Ascher, copyright © 1983. Originally published in *The New York Times.* Reprinted by permission of Rhoda A. Weyr
Agency.

(continued at the back of the book)

ACKNOWLEDGMENTS

This book is not a solitary effort, but a record of conversations and inspirations received from countless people. I can only single out a few who made special efforts to help transform my thoughts into print.

My deepest gratitude to Jonathan Dolger, my literary agent, not only for his intelligent guidance of this book from conception to completion, but for calm assurance, sharp judgment, and valued friendship. To Patricia Soliman, my editor, my appreciation and admiration; her skill with the written word is matched only by her warmth and unique blend of insight and encouragement.

My appreciation to Nancy Friday, whom I met when taping a segment for the "Tomorrow" show in 1980. She interviewed me on a topic that is strongly developed in her book *My Mother/My Self:* young women's conflicts about their own sexuality and how this ambivalence is apparent in their attitudes toward and use (or non-use) of contraception. We agreed that the Swept Away phenomenon still was pervasive.

Months later I called Nancy to consult with her about another project I had in mind. She advised me to postpone it, to write this book, as it was more important. I thank her for her generous encouragement. She is one of the most stimulating women I have met, and I admire her tremendous contribution to the better understanding of female sexuality.

To my colleagues who gave so generously of their time, I offer thanks: William Fishburn, Beverly Hotchner, Felicia Guest, Elizabeth Canfield. Also, to David Epstein and Timothy Wernette for sharing their thoughts with me. I particularly want to thank Karen Cantrell for her thoughtful reviews and help in crystallizing hazy facts, and for her uncanny ability to put her finger on just the right research source. My gratitude to Michael Carrera for his support and suggestions and to Paul Dearth for getting me on the right track. And to Sol Gordon, my irrepressible source of wit, enthusiasm, ideas, and great plans, my heartfelt thanks.

A special note of appreciation to three people for reading numerous drafts and providing a shot of confidence when spirits got low: Lydia Neumann, whose combination of constructive criticism and intellectual insight was a constant stimulus; Natalie Mackler, whose wise counsel never failed to pinpoint the problem, and whose creative contributions helped give this book depth and substance; and Kay Scott Bard, on whom I could always count for solid advice, good humor, and her special talent for sorting out trees from forests.

To Shannon Cooley, Deborah Hughes Morningstar, and Kate Bennett for their priceless contribution of typing and editorial assistance, and most gratefully to Dorothy Case for her legerdemain in turning scraps of paper into a typed page, and for her unfailing optimistic attitude. A thank-you to Elaine Blair for her skill with syntax and grammar and for getting me through not only my Ph.D. but the final drafts of this book. I owe a debt of gratitude to Dee Ratterree, who made the overwhelmingly significant contribution of making the book more lively and readable.

Appreciation to Susan Albin, Tim Lannan and the clan at James Bowman Associates for keeping the faith.

And special thanks to my family, who were extraordinarily

understanding and supportive throughout this whole project. But most of all, I thank the women and men I interviewed or surveyed who contributed their time, thoughts, and personal experience. Many of them appear disguised in these pages, under fictitious names, but their contributions enriched this book.

My task which I am trying to achieve is,
by the power of the written word to make
you hear, to make you feel—it is,
before all, to make you see. That—
and no more, and it is everything. If
I succeed, you shall find here . . .
encouragement, consolation, fear, charm—
all you demand—and, perhaps, also that
glimpse of truth for which you have
forgotten to ask.

JOSEPH CONRAD

This book is dedicated to my friend and spouse, Bob,
for keeping my feet planted firmly on the ground
while cheering me on to reach for the stars.

CONTENTS

AUTHOR'S NOTE

To insure *Swept Away* doesn't collect any cobwebs, I've updated statistics and information to reflect new developments in the field of female and male sexuality. For example, in the short interval between the first edition and this one, the AIDS crisis has cast a threatening shadow over our lives. Clearly, the freewheeling days of having sex with someone you've just met, or know only casually, are over—it is just too risky. Now, this doesn't signal a hasty retreat to the sexual mores of the fifties—chastity and Good Girlness. It does, however, make it even more compelling to make intelligent choices about sexuality, and not deny responsibility for our sexual selves by being Swept Away. In short, the consequences of Swept Away expectations and behavior are now life-threatening—contacting AIDS—as well as life-damaging—facing an unintended pregnancy, getting our egos bruised and our hearts stomped on.

On the plus side, the brass ring to be caught by tossing aside our love-junkie, rose-colored glasses has never looked better, brighter. The prize is this: We free ourselves to live and love as smart women, to twirl sprightly into the flirtatious dance of the sexes with a clear sighting on who we are and what we want.

I would like to acknowledge the person who made this revision possible, my remarkable editor, Laura Yorke, who is everything an author dreams about having in an editor—competent, smart, and witty to boot. Bouquets of heartfelt appreciation, Laura.

One of the most gratifying experiences of being an author has been savoring the responses I've had from the readers of *Swept Away*. I especially want to thank the many many women and men who wrote, called, and gently took me aside at my seminars to tell me how much this book helped them put their "ducks in a row." Your kudos have meant the most to me.

INTRODUCTION

The bright and sunny June day I walked up to the dais at the University of New Mexico and received the scrap of sheepskin that declared me a Bachelor of Arts was my own private Independence Day. I must have been one of the proudest people on that platform: marriage, four children, and a recent divorce had intervened over the long fifteen years between my high school graduation and this precious piece of paper. Along the way, I faced the daily grind of raising the kids and making ends meet; I did my class assignments in the odd hours I could steal from my family, late at night or first thing in the morning. The entire order of my world shifted in what seemed like a brief and tremendously exciting time, for I was one of the legions of women whose life was substantially changed by reading *The Feminine Mystique;* once I got the notion that a woman's place was anywhere a man could go and depended solely on what she could accomplish, I enthusiastically forged ahead. I'll always be grateful to Betty Friedan for the improvement she wrought in my life: I hope this book is one way to repay the debt.

After graduation, I went out into the world, found my first (real) job, fell in love, and remarried.

Then, in the early 1970s, my previous struggles were rewarded and my career launched when I was chosen, one of a handful of educators, to attend the University of Pennsylvania's prestigious and revolutionary program in sex education and family planning, with courses on campus and a lot of field work.

At the end of the decade, I was at another pivotal point. With the offer of a perfect job in hand, although I had to swallow really hard, I moved to New York City. I still had some tag ends on my dissertation to complete, so I was busier than ever. Finally, a rite of passage was over: dressed in a long black gown with velvet stripes on the sleeves, I stood to receive the silver and ice-blue satin hood—symbolizing Doctor of Philosophy—placed on my shoulders. My job became exhilarating, the culmination of my professional hopes: it offered me the chance to create sex education programs for women that would really inform them and make a difference in their lives.

But my personal life was in flux, a reflection of the lives of women all around me. We were taking stock, inventorying our gains and losses accrued in that decade of movements, rights, and revolutions. Second marriage now in limbo, separated, living alone for the first time in my life (I had gone from daughter to wife to mother), I found myself in a singles world which was light-years away from any experience I'd had before. The jolts and surprises of my new life gave me food for thought and material for this book.

The time and distance I had from my husband allowed me, and him, to think clearly and rationally about what we wanted from our relationship. With a fresh outlook, we renewed our commitment to each other, although my work kept us the width of the continent apart over the next few years.

So the last decade has, for me, been a particularly eventful one: I've changed the way I look at the world, at relationships, even at myself. I've criss-crossed the country a hundred times in various capacities in my career as a sex educator—lecturing, teaching, conducting workshops in human sexuality. I've come into contact with literally thousands of men and women, listened to myriad questions and discussions on sex and its role in our lives. Out of this abundance of experience, I began to understand that a common priority for men and women is to achieve better relationships that include sex.

I discovered early in my career that being an expert in the functions of the human sexual apparatus is only a fraction of the knowledge I need. I've known the mechanics for years: the determined, arduous journey of the spermatazoa, the monthly miracle of the ovum, the elegant mathematics of meiosis and mitosis. I can (and will) describe in minute detail the stages of arousal—male and female—from increased pulse rate through orgasmic spasm. But I rarely get asked a question about anatomy: instead I'm perpetually bombarded with questions about love.

Again and again I've been taken aback at the lack of connection between a woman's love fantasy and the world's reality. I'm alarmed by the frequency of unhappy endings to storybook beginnings. I'm appalled by the number of unwanted, unplanned pregnancies in this country. I'm saddened by my sense that something isn't working. There is still so much pain, so many problems over sex, even given the current liberal attitudes toward contraception, sex education, premarital sex. Yet the thorny truth as I hear it in innumerable voices across the land is that sex seems to "screw up" relationships.

> When he looked deep into my eyes and murmured "I want you," I was swept away by his passion. I thought it was special, love. But when he avoided my eyes and muttered "I'll call you" on his way out the door the next morning, I knew it wasn't love. I'd just been screwed again.
>
> *Nancy, 34*

Women today seem to have fallen into a tangle of failed relationships, sexual misapprehension, and general, gnawing discontent. There's an abyss between our expectations and our realities. Despite the sexual revolution, the pill, slogans of sisterhood, and media assurance that "we've come a long way," we are still not sexually free or emotionally satisfied.

Let me be very clear at the outset—I do not blame feminism or the so-called sexual revolution for messing up women's sex lives. I don't have any sentimental longing for the prehistoric days before the women's movement. None at all. It was *not* the best of times, or the good old days, no matter how nostalgic we may wax over the songs, the fashions, the simpler divisions of the proper behavior for each sex—men-as-men, women-as-women: hard/soft, aggressive/passive. It was an insidious time for individual men and individual women confined by a society hell-bent on conformity. Few women who have a choice would want to return to a time of only one choice disguised as three: *"Kinder, Kirche, Küchen."* But what I've discovered is that the morass of confusion and lack of understanding about modern sexuality, especially female sexuality, has set the stage to create a strategy for dealing with sex that women almost universally seek refuge in: a strategy I call Swept Away.

1

A COUNTERFEIT EMOTION

THE ROMANCE CONNECTION

I glanced at my watch and then out at the river that winds through the heart of San Antonio, watching the tour boats glide slowly by. I was waiting for my friend Joyce to meet me at a small café for brunch: we hadn't seen each other for a year, since she'd moved back to Texas to practice law. And it began to look as though I wouldn't see her now: she was very late, and I was nervous because the seminar I was giving—my excuse to visit San Antonio—was the first of the afternoon. I was nearly out of my chair when Joyce breezed in and dropped down in the chair across from me, looking slightly frazzled.

"I'm so sorry about being late," she said in her charming Southern drawl. "But I have an excuse that will fry your ears!" She leaned over the table and whispered, "I hadn't been home since I left for work yesterday morning, so I had to make a detour to change clothes. I've been up all night making love. This time it's the real thing. I have finally fallen totally in love. I know it's sudden, does it seem crazy? But it's love."

She subsided momentarily as the waitress filled our coffee cups, then launched into the details of this newfound romance. "Last night I had to go to a statewide lawyers' meeting. During happy hour, I spotted this incredible-looking man: tall, sandy-colored hair, Ivy League and outdoorsy, so I introduced myself. We hit it off right away, and when the bar closed, he suggested we continue our conversation over dinner. We took a long drive out to a great barbecue place, had terrific ribs, corn bread and plenty of beer—a real hill-country feast. As the night progressed, so did we, and I ended up back at his hotel room. I know, I know . . . I'm usually too uptight for one-night stands, but this is different. He's so gentle and sensitive—I've never made love like that before. I'm really carried away . . . totally smitten!"

I found my mind drifting, my senses turned inward as I fantasized scene after passionate scene—dancing cheek to cheek, satin sheets a-tumble, the surf roaring across entwined bodies; but something brought me up short with a premonitory shudder. Instead of feeling exhilarated at her pleasure, I was strangely discomfited. And as I thought over the episode later in the cool and neutral confines of my hotel room, I realized that Joyce's story had really disturbed me. "Carried away," "head over heels," "blinded by love," "swept away." Do the words we use to describe the state of being in love really tell a different story, perhaps one of confusion, disorientation, even mental anguish? I gave myself a shake, and a reprimand: morbid, jealous, I accused.

I went home, my seminar over, and didn't think about Joyce for a couple of weeks. Then a phone call, and the ominous feeling I'd had was confirmed.

"I spent three days and nights with him," she wept. "For all of the candlelight, and wine, and romance, and *great* sex, it was really only an extended one-nighter for him. I feel so stupid, and so used."

I sighed and tried to console her with maxims comparing men to fish in the sea in both number and availability, but she wasn't convinced and neither was I. Not convinced, but I *was* alerted. I began to pay sharper attention to the signs and signals around me, and slowly but surely, as I amassed material and stories, I formed first a theory and then a certainty about the *way* in which women handle (and mishandle) sexual encounters.

REPORTS FROM THE BATTLEFIELD

It was devastating. I met this man through a mutual friend, the chemistry was there, and after a couple of days we were telling each other we were in love and talking about living together. I couldn't bear to be parted from him, I didn't feel complete alone. He danced away after about eight weeks, and I felt terrible. I never got to know what happened. I felt disgusted and wanted to burn my sheets and swear off men. It took me a year to get over it.

Leslie, 38

I met Fred at a conference. I was recently divorced and I was "skin-starved" and desperately in need of intimacy. We started meeting each other once a month in romantic cities. No brief-cases, no telephones—and no future. It turned out he was a workaholic who only saw the light of day our one weekend a month, and I had fallen madly in love with a man who didn't really exist.

Jennifer, 34

Ah, there he was, across the room. The man a friend had said was "for me." I had recently broken up with a long-time lover and I had been lonelier than I thought possible. This new man was everything I wanted—warm, funny, sexy, same religion, similar interests (except *he* liked sports). My heart wouldn't stop pounding. We had little time together, but had he asked then, I would have changed my *whole* life for him. We spent the night together, then he went back to his home on the other side of the country. A year and a half later, I still have pangs when I'm in the restaurant we went to. It hurts sometimes. I feel foolish . . .

but without risking falling madly in love I would have missed a lovely experience.

Joan, 26

Three stories, three women's fumbling attempts to find love, a solid relationship. And only three of thousands upon thousands. What went wrong? The pattern is visible to the naked eye, it doesn't require a microscope: a woman meets a man, "falls in love," has sex, and falls deeper in love—but doesn't necessarily *find* love. That seems to be the way women handle sexual encounters: passionately, but misguidedly. My certainty of this pattern has increased a hundredfold in researching and writing, but it's taken years of sorting out to discover *why* we do this, *why* we need so desperately to be Swept Away.

A FANTASY REFLEX

The central fact—and fault—of women's sexuality is that all too often we deny responsibility for it: we wrap our desire in a cloak of romance, need "love" in order to have sex. This one simple ruse, the demand to be Swept Away, is so pervasive and so complicated that major battles in the sexual revolution are still being fought.

I was slow to arrive at the recognition that something was amiss about our never-ending urge to infuse romantic passion into our lives. The consequences weren't readily apparent. At first I only felt uneasy as I unraveled my *own* need to be carried away, swept off my feet. But I discovered that women pay a price. We're confusing what we want with what society says we should be, and the complications that ensue are leading us into unfulfilling relationships. Our energy is sapped, our spunk is gone. A woman's lack of sexual confidence overflows into the rest of her life; it makes her passive, dependent.

Swept Away is a sexual strategy, a coping mechanism, which allows women to be sexual in a society that is, at best, still ambivalent about, and at worst, condemnatory of female sexuality. It is a tactic, employed unconsciously by women to get what they want—a man, sexual pleasure—without having to pay the price of being labeled sleazy or promiscuous. Swept Away is, consequently, a counterfeit emotion, a fraud, a disguise of our true erotic feelings which we've been socialized to describe as romance.

One of a woman's most pervasive fantasies is being Swept Away by the man of her dreams. Fireworks explode, waves pound, knees buckle, two hearts beat as one. (Until the morning after!) It's embedded in our culture, this notion of the thrilling ecstasy of passion. You can see it everywhere: in songs, movies, literature, advertising.

Obviously, it's the mainstay of romance writers. Two examples from the reams of paperbacks jamming the stands: "His lips came down on hers and swept away her fears and unhappiness";[1] and, "When Britt took the assignment to cover Philippe, she was only trying to ensure the coveted staff position at *La Ré Bue* magazine. But soon she is swept away by an overwhelming attraction, suddenly nothing matters."[2] One publisher launched a romance series proclaiming, "You'll Be Swept Away!" Newspaper headlines scream "Liz Swept Off Her Feet," or Debra or Brooke or whoever. *Glamour* magazine recently asked, "were you ever bowled over by something other than flowers or candy . . . a wonderful, unexpected gesture that made you believe in love all over again . . . were you ever SWEPT AWAY?" Then, it issued an invitation to submit a real-life romantic story (350 words or less) with $50.00 going to those that got published.[3] *Swept Away* was even the title of a Lina Wertmuller movie (a tale of an independent woman who after being shipwrecked on a lonely island with her servant turns into marshmallow when he becomes her domineering lover). Singers warble endlessly about trips to the moon on gossamer wings and going out of our heads.

We cut our teeth on tales of women carried away by the passion of the moment to a world that will last happily-ever-after. We develop a fantasy reflex. At the slightest hint that Cupid hovers nearby, we begin to conjure up visions. Clinging to a dark-eyed, silent man as we gallop together across pale moonlit sands on the back of his silvery Arabian stallion . . . Sailing into a technicolor sunset in azure waters, a virile skipper at the helm . . . Nestled fur-clad in the back of the longest, glossiest limousine imaginable with a suave, icy-blue-eyed movie star whispering sweet nothings into our ear . . . Rhett Butler catching Scarlett O'Hara into his arms and sweeping her up that grand staircase to ecstasy.

We are constantly bombarded with the message that romance is the ultimate goal for a woman and the only acceptable rationale for her desire. As soon as a woman feels a physical tug for a man, she transforms it into a romantic drama —wondrously, joyously she begins to drift into love *because* she is aroused. Transported and transformed, she becomes Swept Away.

But when a relationship begins because of a fantasy and not because of a clear-eyed assessment of who the woman is, who the man is, and what they each want and expect, illusions are bound to crumble. We exchange the brief moments of euphoria we get when we "fall in love" for long hours of depression, anger, and hostility when an encounter doesn't follow the fictitious course we've plotted.

We are flesh-and-blood women; we don't live in a romantic novel. We live in a world populated by men who cannot be counted on to play the role of gallant hero in the passionate script we dreamed up.

So the romantic aura is false and confusing. We become deceived about the meaning of our experience. In refusing to acknowledge the unique claim of our sexual natures, we refuse to be fully responsible. We hand our sexuality over to the men in our lives, make them responsible for our submission to them. We become dependent, passive. We won't have sex unless we're seduced, driven *out of control*. What we can't control, we can't be blamed for. We use this syndrome to inject the thrill of romance into our lives, lives still subject to the constraints imposed on us because we are women, the female gender.

This isn't a new theory, or an unsupported one. Whenever I told friends and colleagues the title of this book, it brought instant recognition. No one needed a lengthy explanation: it was understood. Educators, therapists, psychologists, and sociologists have isolated the behavior: it's an identified, recognized aspect of sexual interplay. Bits and pieces that contribute to my theory have lurked in the literature of human sexuality for the last twenty years.[4]

In textbooks, there are dozens of references to how women are trapped into denying their sexuality. For example, James McCary, in his college standard *Human Sexuality*, found that a woman must be "carried away" to avoid "planning" sex.[5] Noted sociologist Greer Litton Fox in her research on the cultural norms controlling female sexuality found that for an unmarried woman to allow herself sexual intercourse she must be "so uncontrollably in love as to be virtually swept away by the spontaneous and unrestrainable passions of that particular moment."[6] In the field of family planning, it was acknowledged early on, but not defined as such. In a 1971 study for Planned Parenthood, for instance, Pamela Lowry was aware of it when she wrote, "Years of indoctrination with the 'nice girls don't' theory make many young women unable to accept intercourse unless they are 'swept away' or seduced," but she didn't focus it.[7]

It took Nancy Friday to identify the problem and give it a name. Examining, in her book *My Mother/My Self*, the way women began their sexual lives, unprotected by contraception, she said, "There is this absolutely uncanny, almost suicidally foolish manner in which women enter sex. What it says is that the solution to our problem is not to have to face it at all. It is the great Swept Away phenomenon."[8]

A FIRST STEP

I want to know that I play with a full deck—that I understand
what sexual messages I'm giving out and what sexual messages
mean when they are returned by men.

Patricia, 27

I am convinced that only when our culture comfortably accepts the fact that sex is an integral part of everyone's life will
women be able to deal with being female and sexual without
being Swept Away. Examining the way we approach sexuality
in a world of enduring double standards and double messages, I have no grand theories of salvation other than self-
knowledge. I hope only to take apart these insidious restraints, gut them of their power and influence, so that women
can see where the conflict and ambivalence come from. I want
us to understand the roots of our behavior: historical, psychological, cultural, biological.

My primary concern is to provide the opportunity for
women to look at their own sexual conflicts and design their
own solutions based on intelligent consideration; I want men
to have the opportunity to understand why women act the
way they do. For both sexes, I want to afford the opportunity
of "playing with a full deck."

To that end, I have gathered material for over a decade. I've
talked to professionals and experts in psychology, social biology, sociology, anthropology, and my own field, human sexuality. I have compiled and interpreted hundreds of pages of
material that I've garnered, tabulated statistics, and run down
references.

But in the final analysis, recognizing the force of women's
need to be Swept Away is best achieved by letting people
themselves talk about their emotions and behavior. I've sent
out hundreds of questionnaires, conducted workshops, taped
interviews. Women have called me from all over the country

—friends and friends of friends as well as total strangers—and sent me long hand-written letters, pouring out their hearts. This book is their book, these concerns their concerns.

Until now, no one has taken a really close look at how the need to be swept off our feet makes us feel about ourselves, at how it's damaging and limiting our lives and the lives of men we try to relate to in this fumbling, rudimentary way. There has been scant attention paid to the pervasive, destructive way it is rooted in our culture and how deeply it influences the way we think about men and sex and love. And never before have so many women told, in their own voices, of pain and confusion, of the wretched unhappiness being Swept Away can ultimately cause, despite its initial razzle-dazzle.

This book is about sex and power and change. Old messages, new misunderstandings. Where we came from, how we got here, where to go now. It's a field report from the battlefronts of the sexual revolution all around the country.

We thought the sexual revolution would free us, make us equal to men, explain men to us. Twenty years later, we feel neither free nor equal. Change has always frightened some people, made others angry, invigorated a stalwart few. The line between liberation and loneliness gets blurred at times. Men and women have been fighting the battle of the sexes since time immemorial, but they've nevertheless managed a lot of love and devotion and companionship, too. I'm confident that, with a little patience, a lot of insight, and true desire, we can work things out.

2

THE VEILED CONTRACT

Once in a while I want to be wooed, swept off my feet by some small tender gesture. Men seem oblivious to the finer points of love and romance nowadays. I would like to feel comfortable with my lover, to like him as a person, to have established some sort of relationship and be on the road to becoming friends before making love. I find this impossible to achieve and I blame it on too easy sex. No violets, no heart-shaped boxes of chocolate, no troubadours serenading you with songs of love at sunrise—just sex.

Joan, 32

Sex *is* the cutting edge of a man and woman's relationship. It is metamorphic, alters the way we think and feel about ourselves; it permeates our emotions, the way we relate to a man. We want sex to be a plus in our lives, to enrich our relationships. But, like Joan, women are feeling that they are not getting what they need. There's a gap between old rituals and new expectations that not only has not been bridged, too often it's not even acknowledged: *when a woman has sex with a man she feels he is beholden to her.*

As much as we would like to deny it, we still believe, at least a little, in the old axiom that sex is a beautiful gift a woman bestows upon a man. This leads us into expecting something special to happen in its aftermath—perhaps, at first, some simple display of affection, flowers, a sweet card, dinner; then later we expect love, devotion, invested time, a future commitment. By continuing to operate with these expectations, we're unwittingly enacting an ancient ritual: offering the promise of sex with us in exchange for the security a man can provide. While this contract has been rapidly changing, it still exists, but not overtly: it is hidden, disguised, veiled.

SEXUAL BARGAINING

I have a nagging feeling that sex is something I use in exchange for a man's commitment. There are still times when I seriously doubt whether I have won very much in the sexual revolution. I still feel like men and women don't share sex: men "get some," women "put out."

                                                            Pamela, 24

Pamela's words—putting out, getting—cause a shudder, a chill, a feeling of repulsion. They have a hostile sound, the ring of the marketplace. We hate the thought of sex as a transaction, a trade-off. But Pamela isn't alone. Women are beginning to understand that at the root of their underlying dissatisfaction about sexual freedom is something substantial, embedded. We idealize the free exchange of love between a man and a woman, but our intuition and experience combine to remind us that this is a rarely realized compact. Buried in the recesses of our memories are years of messages telling us that sex is our most important asset *if* rationed, *if* kept out of reach. We don't act consciously on this powerful idea; it operates like a muffled drumbeat signaling us to be careful, not to squander sex or we won't be appreciated, valued, held dear.

For some women this means their heads tell them they are

sexually free, but their hearts say otherwise. Other women seem oblivious to the roots of their fears about being fully sexual. Others get occasional glimpses of what underlies their uneasiness with their sexual relationships. But once articulated we recognize it, no matter how reluctantly: it is the fear that we can't freely share sex with a man without losing something in the bargain.

"I have a real 'oh, damn' hangover after I have sex with a man I didn't know that well. It changes everything too fast," is the way Diane, a woman I interviewed, expressed her misgivings about the new sexual freedom. She added, "Men ask, 'Why wait?' but they act differently toward you after sex, as if you're less valuable somehow. I hate to play sex games, but I feel I'm going to have to change my act, play at least a little harder to get so the man will appreciate what he's got."

Once a woman does have sex with a man, it's as Diane suspects: she doesn't gain power, she loses it. Potential, in this case, was the power base: actuality destroys it. A woman who wrote me offered this rationale: "Men are still trapped in their primitive roles as hunter, caveman. So when they don't engage in a battle, if only a mock one, to have sex with a woman they don't feel they have to pay homage to her." She sent me a poem of an unknown twelfth-century poet, one I cringe at reading because of the insight it affords into our own twentieth century:

> What is freely supplied me
> I shudder at,
> But if aught is denied me,
> I long for that
> With constant mind
> She who's effusive
> I flee;
> The girl who's elusive
> Suits me. . . .[1]

Over and over I hear variations on the theme. "I would have liked the relationship to continue for a while, but once I said yes to sex, it was goodbye," a forty-one-year-old nurse told me. Her experience was a parody of the give-and-take of intimacy. No matter how experienced a man is, sex is an event, and one which reiterates his entry into manhood. We are taught that when a women first has intercourse, she "loses" her virginity, the man "wins" her maidenhead. A woman's loss is defined as a man's gain. This feeling continues long after first intercourse: coitus for a man repeats his initiation rites; for a woman it reiterates her sense of loss.

Imbued with a sense of having lost something irretrievable, women harbor the inarticulate but deep need to have evidence that they are valued, appreciated by the man with whom they have sex. Linda, a thirty-year-old realtor, exacts an emotional toll. "Does he really like *me*? I always wonder, no matter how terrific the sex, if I'm just a physical release or if he feels something special for *me*," she told me. The issue for Linda is apparently not whether *she* feels something special for the man she's sleeping with. The bargain here is, "I gave you sex. In return, you owe it to me to treat me as special, to give me at least some of your time, attention, devotion." The men Linda sleeps with become "lovers." They are set up to abide by different expectations than friends. Friends do things based on generosity and mutual good will; lovers, in this case, because they are obligated.

We use sex as a measure. We say, "I shouldn't have had sex on the first date," or "That's the fourth time we've had sex, and he still hasn't said he likes me." We worry that if we waste it, we won't get proper remuneration—another date, the verbal talisman of "I love you"—in return. Can you imagine a man worrying, "I shouldn't have sex until the third date"? Much as we despise the notion that women have to ration sex to get what they want from a man, *we dole out sex*, use it as a reward, withhold it as punishment. "I turn my back on my husband in bed if he flirts with another woman at a party," wrote Gwen, twenty-six, a social worker. "Even if I'm horny, I make up my mind—no sex. He can try all he wants, but he can't get me interested. I won't budge." Demeaning, but a fact of life. Because we are confused about the long-term rewards of freely given sex, we need reassurance that a man will love us beyond the immediate need to have sex.

Men don't seem to experience this dilemma: sex is something a man pursues because he wants to, because he's conditioned all his life to get sex, because it's physically satisfying. Men don't expect rewards other than orgasm. Larry, twenty-seven, put it frankly, if humorously: "The only thing you should expect in return for sex is a kid or a social disease." His comment may not tickle our funny bone, but one thing is clear: the sexual revolution signaled to many men the end of decades of obligation to the women they have sex with.

THE OLD EXCHANGE

To be blunt, sex has historically been a commodity. It's a valuable source of power in a relationship. Traditionally, it was clearly understood that regular sexual relations were the sine qua non of the commitment between a man and a woman. A woman's most reliable currency was the *potential* of sex, and it was expected that she would use it to secure a man's lifelong devotion. For a man, having sex with a woman was not frivolous; he was then obligated to honor her, protect her, provide her with worldly comforts. The contract was that a woman would take care of the man's needs and he would provide her and their children with support and status. His domain was economic, hers was emotional.[2]

This notion of sexual bartering is rooted in a society where resources have so far been unequally distributed and men have the lion's share. Social anthropologist Kenneth Eckhardt found that "when individuals possess different goods, they will establish and exchange relationships in order to satisfy personal needs."[3] Eckhardt described a society where males dominate the political, economic, and social resources and where women want and need to gain access to these resources. Sexual power is then the female commodity: her biological ability to bear society's offspring. This power has always aroused both fear and awe among men, because while a man can impregnate, he can't give birth to his child. Children—in both a cultural and personal sense—are manifest evidence of a man's ability to procreate, the essence of his maleness. Offspring also lend a kind of immortality: a man's progeny march into the future, continuing and propagating his name, and a part of himself. But a man wants to ensure that his investment is indeed in *his* genes. Marrying a virgin bride, then, was a sort of hereditary insurance policy. Virginity for a woman was her blue-chip stock, her trade-off for the security of the marriage contract, and her assurance to the man that she wasn't pregnant with another man's child.

Society's ever vigilant control over female sexuality can be traced to a central fact: *maternity is certain; paternity, uncertain.* (Even today sophisticated blood tests can prove only that a certain man is *not* the father. The mother identifies the father on the birth certificate. If there is a dispute, the burden of proof is on the male.) Thus virginity was culturally assigned great worth, and women learned to guard it accordingly. And to guard virginity is to withhold sex, a maneuver any shrewd trader can tell you will enhance the value of a commodity (and a habit that persists long after virginity is gone).

In this social system, marriage is the only proper matrix for childrearing. So a man must marry, but he seeks a woman who appeals to him on an emotional basis. Women use a combination of mystery, glamour, and flattery to land a willing mate. And, "women are socialized to keep sex in short supply while men are socialized to demand sex. This creates a gap between supply and demand, giving the woman the bargaining edge."[4] It's a society remarkably like our own until the last twenty years or so, and one whose vestiges are still dramatically with us.

You can hear echoes of the old exchange between a man and

a woman orchestrated in our wedding customs today. "Who gives this woman to this man?" The father of the bride performs this ritual. Brides wear white (symbol of purity), bridesmaids flutter about as "handmaidens" while flower girls scatter petals in the path of the maiden bride. Vows include fidelity "until death us do part," and the bride's family pays for the whole show—a custom directly traced to the ancient bridal dowries. In some religious rituals, the man publicly pledges he will provide his wife and their children-to-be with lifetime support. This is hardly a romantic view of the relationship, but it should go a long way toward explaining the historical persistence of marriage: beyond the rice-throwing celebration, marriage is a *civil contract*, and as such is regulated by law.[5] Society has always peeked over the shoulder of the happy couple.

Even as late as the 1940s, marriage in this country was routinely viewed as an exchange of a male's wages for a female's sexual and domestic services, with security, stability, and offspring the desired outcome. Not until World War II, when women entered the labor force in unheard-of numbers and learned to be wage earners—providers—did the equation begin to change. Then the war ended, men returned from the battlefields to the factories, and women were once again relegated to hearth and home. Henrietta Homemaker displaced Rosie the Riveter: woman's work was no longer welding and winning the bread but rearing children and keeping house. And for another decade, women subsided back into the confinement of economic dependency.

If the concept of exchange by contract seems outmoded, think back not even fifteen years ago to one of the most famous liaisons of a generation, bound by a highly debated document. Jacqueline Kennedy and Aristotle Onassis: the titillation and shock that attended their marriage were occasioned less by the disparity in their ages and life-styles—after all, that wealth and power deserve youth and beauty is still an acknowledged axiom—than by the rumors of the existence of a bedroom clause in their marriage contract, a clause that was said to have suggested, or at least hinted that "shared bedroom time" would balance off a yacht and an island named Skorpios.

We can cry "special circumstances" about the Onassis marriage. We can offer up careers and credit cards, earned status and "equal" relationships to deny the need women have to barter over sex. We can try to consign those calculated transactions to the dim mists of history. Nobody likes to face up to the trading aspects of an erotic alliance; it seems so crude. But we're not able to completely dismiss their existence. Every woman I know is discomfited by her inability to deny—deep down—her instinct that sex always has strings attached.

CATCHING THE BOUQUET

Hear what Patricia, a woman in her early twenties, told me: "Why bother investing time, caring, and money in a relationship that is going nowhere? If I really like a guy I can't see just dating him or living together to have a good time. There has to be at least the potential that we can carve out a life together." Women want a serious relationship to have some glue, something binding it together. And until something else is invented to fill the bill, that something is marriage. Sheila, a magazine editorial assistant, observes why that is so: "I think women still get married for security (as incredible as this is, what with the laws the way they are, and divorce rates as high as they are) because it is expected. Socialization tells a girl early on that marriage is what makes a woman. Or women get married because a relationship doesn't count as much without it —no coincidence after the first two reasons." But the popular wisdom that a woman is better off married puts a strain on women trying to develop a life of their own, enjoy sexual pleasure for its own sake—it goes to the core of a woman's need to define relationships in terms of a future.

More women are single now than ever before. And society is more supportive of single people. Back in 1950 when the "procreation ethic" was in full swing, a University of Michigan poll asked what Americans would think of someone who had decided never to marry. The answers were adamant: sick, antisocial, selfish. By 1976, sentiments had flip-flopped; now most people said it was all right not to want to get married, even some, both men and women, said they would be *positively* impressed with someone electing to remain single.[6] Beside the groundswell of support for being single, marriage has apparently lost its overwhelming appeal for some women. Robert Ferrigno, a newspaper staff writer, gives reasons why: "In this culture, marriage is a better deal for a man than for a woman, particularly now that so many women have incomes from working outside the house. Men not only get the nurturing environment most women are raised to provide, they also have an economic partner. Plus easily available sex. All this, in addition to the fact that, in most relationships, the man is the domineering partner."[7] But as tempting as it might be to say that matrimony no longer springs eternal in the hearts of independent, intelligent, talented women who value their self-reliance and freedom, it would be off-base. There has been no wholesale retreat from the altar.

We are the marrying kind. Ninety-three percent of all Americans do marry sometime in their lives; after divorce, one in four remarry. While the number of unmarried couples has more than tripled since 1970, they are only 4 percent of all couples.[8] Most men and women surveyed say they expect to get married someday. In fact, marriage as an institution appears to be enjoying a new vogue. People who have never been to a wedding, much less a bridal shower, find themselves responding to engraved invitations, visiting the department store bridal registry to select the right china or silver pattern, putting on their Sunday best, and raising a champagne glass in enthusiastic toast to the newlyweds.

Arlene Saluter of the Census Bureau explains that couples

are postponing marriage in favor of an education and getting a career started, "returning to the pattern of the timing of first marriage that characterized the United States in the early decades of this century."[9] It was only for a brief period, in the late 1940s and 1950s, that couples married younger and younger. But the heart of the matter here is that, while we are waiting just a *little* longer, most people still get married in their twenties. The newlywed bride's median age is 22.5 years, the groom's 25.2 years. By the age of 26.6 three-quarters of all women have married. As for men, three-fourths of them have wed by age 29.4.[10]

Now, I am *not* on the marriage bandwagon; I am not even sure if marriage is ever what it is cracked up to be, or if it ultimately hinders or hurts relationships, adds to or subtracts from our life's happiness. But no matter whether one reveres or scorns the institution of marriage, it is still the only adult relationship that has society's Solid Gold Seal of Approval.

THE BEST YEARS OF OUR LIVES?

Don't underestimate the pressures on a woman to get evidence of a man's commitment to her by tying the nuptial knot; they are relentless. It was a rueful chuckle that rippled through the movie theater when two beautiful young dancers in the film *Flashdance*, while folding laundry in the local laundromat, exchanged confidences about what happened to your relationship with a man after you had sex with him. After considering several scenarios, they, in unison, mimicked the universal warning given to legions of daughters by their worried mothers: "He will *never* marry you!"

Family approval still counts. Shirley, a twenty-nine-year-old administrative assistant who told me she had just gotten engaged, put it this way: "Women generally get married to raise children, share expenses, save money together; have someone they can depend on, someone they can do things with. I can do all these things without getting married if I want to. However, I would have the biggest problem with parental/societal approval. His parents would treat me differently if we decided not to marry, just to live together, and his sisters would feel the same. We probably wouldn't be invited on weekend trips and we could never sleep together on those trips, anyway, if we weren't married, even if we *were* living together. This goes for my parents as well. So my only reason for getting married is really to fit in with our families' expectations so that we can enjoy being with them."

And it isn't just the young. A woman I interviewed told me about a friend of hers who is forty, single, and likes it that way. "She enjoys traveling, visiting people on a whim, and living in her cozy apartment with a view of New York's East River. She has been going with a man for eight years and they have a wonderful relationship. But what do all our mutual friends tell her? 'Annie, he will never marry you. You're wasting the best years of your life.' " Even among the *most* modern, *most* liberal parents of single women in their late thirties you will find heartfelt concern that their daughter won't ever marry.

Marriage, for all its shortcomings to woman's personal growth, historically gave her a position in society that was respected. And let's face it, marriage is still the ultimate game in town, or, in some settings, the only one in which a woman can win status. Even women who live interesting lives on their own see a husband as an added dimension. Liz Smith, the well-known gossip columnist, mused about marriage in a recent magazine interview: "I think it might be fun to marry a terribly glamorous man and blow everyone's mind. People don't like to admit it, but I think a woman's status in New York changes dramatically if she marries someone important. I think it has been a drawback for me to be single." [11]

THE GOLDEN RULE REVISITED

"There should be no mystery why, over the years, women have had a disproportionate investment in marriage," says writer Barbara Ehrenreich. Women's earnings average out to slightly more than $10,000 a year, "nowhere near enough to support a single in a swinging lifestyle, much less a single mother and her children. For most women, the obvious survival strategy has been to establish a claim on some man's more generous wages, i.e. to marry him." [12] In the cold harsh light of economics, women still *need* more from a man than vice versa.

We *are* achieving a foothold in the worlds of business, politics, power. But deep in our hearts we are uncertain, unused to success, sorely lacking in role models. A woman's sense of security *in her own worth* still does not approach a man's. Women at the top of their professions speak of the uncertainty they feel at being on their own. Success feels fragile, transitory. "I feel I'm one of the 'lucky ones,' " Joanne told me. At forty, she heads her own television production company. "I'm bright, I'm achievement-oriented, I got here through fifteen years of hard work, but I still feel like it's luck . . . like a wrong throw of the dice, an unlucky number, an evil eye could change it all. It could all go down the drain."

Women today are still unsure of their capacity to control their own destinies, and their fears are not unfounded. Resources are by no means equally distributed. Women earn less money than men: 40 percent of the total income, in fact, the same ratio as one hundred years ago. But then only 5 percent of the female population was in the work force, compared to 52 percent today. [13] And if 52 percent of women are in the work force, 48 percent *aren't*. Stop here a minute to consider what is meant by "working women" in those breathless stories announcing the dramatic rise in the number of women in the work force. There has been a giant leap in the number of women who work. But single women have always worked, at least until they got married, or until they had a baby. Later on when the children went to school they might take a supplementary job. Or they might not. What has changed in the expensive 1980s is the number of middle-class married women and mothers of young children who now have to work. Yet women are a mere token statistic: 5 percent of executives in management and finance. We still work in pink-collar ghettos —we're 98 percent of all nurses, 98 percent of all receptionists, 97 percent of all secretaries, nearly 100 percent of all domestics. Although we hold more graduate degrees than men, we're more visible in the steno pool than the faculty lounge. And, shockingly, if we get divorced, we can expect our standard of living to plummet for the first year: a man's, on the other hand, rises by 42 percent.[14] And single again, we head up most poor households with children. Our insurance rates are higher and cover less, our Social Security benefits are lower and, needless to say, cover less.

Like Joanne, we know in the fiber of our beings that we're vulnerable, that the world is not an equal place. "Just a man away from welfare" was the way one wife with two young children described her insecurity to me. True, she could support herself and her children, but, she added, "barely." There have been only a few cracks in the truth of that old variation on the Golden Rule: He who has the gold rules. And he usually does.

The dilemma women face trying to reconcile two conflicting expectations—finding security through a man and finding an "equal" male partner—is magnified by the way the problem is treated. To many it is as if the traditional deal—the exchange of a man's financial status for the sexual, compassionate, and maternal services of a woman—never existed. And the problem is further complicated because, while there is no returning to the breadwinner–breadbaker marriage ethic, public consciousness has not come to grips with the fact that it's not even an available deal for all women. It doesn't acknowledge that a lot of us must earn our own living and, in many cases, *be* the family breadwinner.

No wonder we have a hard time relinquishing the one historically assured control we can exercise: sex. "Only when a society has distributed its political, economic and social resources equally between males and females . . . will [they] engage in sexual intercourse primarily for the social and physical satisfaction it provides." [15] While increasing numbers of women will have the option of financial independence, its universality is probably generations away.

THE CHAINS THAT BIND

Marriage had always been jokingly called a "trap" for men, but now, in some quarters, there is less laughter. Marriage, from a male perspective, may still be a good deal, but many see fewer advantages in it than before.

For a man, being single and over thirty no longer renders him suspect of having an unhealthy attachment to his mother, or being eccentric or gay. He may take some criticism from his women friends for his "lack of commitment" and some ribbing at holiday family dinners about his matrimonial intentions, but a misfit he isn't. [16] Men do not have to get married to prove they are men anymore, while women are still compelled into needing commitment from a man by a powerful amalgam of influences—emotions, economics, family, friends, and the ever-present lever of popular opinion. We may not really feel we are nothing without a man, but the pressure from all sides to become permanently attached to one—a good one—sets us up to barter with sex.

"But I think women's situations are changing for the better," says Sheila. "We are less apt to stay virgins in the hope that a man will come along and ask our hand in marriage. We are more likely to assert ourselves in relationships and initiate working on satisfactory sex, or even on more freedom to be alone." Sheila's optimism has some foundation in truth, but we aren't yet enjoying having a sexual relationship for the joy it gives us; we are still far too uneasy about *his* intentions.

SEXUAL DEVALUATION

It usually doesn't take a guy very long to make his move. You're out on a date having fun and all of a sudden Whammo! the big question. "Ya wanna?" I think, "Oh, God, here we go again." If I like him and say yes, the last thing he says is "Adios, sweetie," and that's it. On the other hand, the last time I said no, he said, "I really respect you for saying that." Then he said, "Adios, sweetie," and that was it. Kind of damned if you do, damned if you don't.

Marcy, 22

It's a truly modern dilemma, this "damned if you do, damned if you don't" spirit of sexual encounters. Widespread availability has sent the market value of sex plummeting. If we deplore the notion of sexual bargaining, we're still secretly panicked that nowadays we're left without chips. When a woman strives to put a value on sexual acquiescence, she doesn't always get the results she wants: "yes" may produce nothing more than a pleasant erotic evening. A man's commitment is no longer guaranteed by the gift of sex. And when a woman attempts to increase the value of her "yes" by withholding sex when she feels for some reason that it is inappropriate, when she says "not yet," she may hear what Marcy heard: "Adios, sweetie." It's the newly reduced value of sex, and it's left us uncertain and newly vulnerable.

I think that a majority of the women I've talked to over the last ten years echo the confusion that Evelyn, a nurse from Seattle, voices. "I really hate the idea that, because I'm having sex with a man whom I haven't known for a long, long time, he'll think I don't value myself. But it's hard to know what to do. If you meet a man and date him two or three times and don't have sex, he begins to feel you are either rejecting him or you have serious sex problems. And frankly, I enjoy sex; I need the hugging and the closeness. But I really dread feeling that I could turn into, in his eyes, an easy lay, a good-time girl. I want men to see me as a grown-up woman who has the same right as they do to make sexual choices."

THE NEW CONTRACT

Women sense the persistence of sex as a commodity, and this creates a conflict. We feel that simply to "have" sex is reckless. As our *only*—or at least most powerful—asset, how can we not conserve it, or barter with it wisely? But we must also take the edge off trying to make the best deal, because straightforward, cold appraisal of the market is directly counter to all the messages we receive about women giving their all for love. Sex can be a high-risk factor; we can lose so much if we have sex too easily, too soon, with the "wrong" kind of man. We know we must be careful about whom we love and when we love.

Equally frightening, if sex is not such valuable merchandise anymore, what *do* we have to offer? How to reconcile these contradictions, how to somehow walk a tightrope over the abyss to the safe haven of a loving man's arms on the other side?

We "have" sex, but we tell ourselves it's not *just* sex, it's love. We tell ourselves that this moment of passion will lead to others because it's special, and therefore we're special. We deny ambivalence, shunt aside feelings of loss, indulge in the physical desire that drives us. *And we revalue this physical impulse, the drive for sex, by investing it with love.*

Unable to face the cold nature of a sexual bargain, unwilling to admit that a sexual encounter may be nothing more, socialized by centuries of experience to view sex as our major attribute, yet living with the modern-day messages and mores of the sexual revolution, we fall back on "love." No one is immune. Judith, a clinical psychologist, described a typical sexual scenario that she went through after her divorce.

> I would look at a new lover and silently pray, "Please let this work out well!" I tried to enchant each appealing man by being the most romantic lady ever—candlelight dinners were my specialty. As I look back on that ridiculous date-around time of my life, I realize I was just frantic and so I tried to make each affair be the special one, the final culmination of my true love dreams.

If sex is everywhere, and nothing special, love is still a one-of-a-kind experience, the "real" thing. The old contract of sex for security has been invalidated, so we've tried to rewrite it, adding a rider: sex equals love.

What could be wrong with a contract that provides a woman with a loving experience? It's wonderful, that tug of romance, the glow a woman feels when a charming, sexy, caressing man concentrates all his energies on her.

Unfortunately, it's a contract only women have signed, and one of which men are often unaware. But it's a contract by which—for reasons we will look at—women feel bound.

At the first sign of sexual arousal, women set up the love fantasy: "I've never gone to bed with a man without caring for him. I always feel 'this man, this experience, is special.' When it finally sinks in that this was 'special' only to me, I could kick myself for being such a dimwit. Wouldn't you think I'd stop doing this to myself?" asked Pam, a thirty-three-year-old writer. It's a counterfeit emotion, a fraud: "This special man, this unique experience." It's doomed to leave a woman unfulfilled, disappointed, and vulnerable to what she perceives as rejection. It leads her to deny the true nature of her encounter, and not to enjoy it for what it was: a purely pleasurable physical exchange. Her assumption was based on a false premise: he loves me *because* we had sex. Unclear about the dynamics of the relationship, she's made a bad bargain: looking for deep and mutual love, she's let herself be Swept Away into self-delusion.

3

CROSSED WIRES, MIXED MESSAGES
THE LOVE/SEX DILEMMA

A CASUAL AFFAIR?

"Sex, he said it was *only* sex." Sara greeted me in pain and disbelief as I stood in the doorway of her apartment. Sara is my shining example of a 1980s woman who has it all: a wildly successful career in television; a wonderful man, one who is prosperous himself, and who is, her female friends privately agree, a huggy hunk of a man. It took me a minute to control my impulse to scream "Mark, you rat, you" and turn instead to comforting my heartbroken friend. I led her inside, fixed her a large tot of brandy, and set myself to listen while Sara unburdened herself.

It was a story as old as time—the sexual peccadillos of the traveling man. Sara and Mark have lived together for seven years. Over that time he had traveled consistently on business for a national firm, and just as consistently had been having affairs with women in different parts of the country.

"How did you find out?" I asked.

Sara flushed and held her breath for a minute, then, sighing deeply, she began, "I'm ashamed to admit it, but I did something terrible. I opened a letter addressed to Mark. I don't know what drew me to that particular one. Maybe I was unconsciously suspicious. Anyway, I was sorting the mail—a letter for me, a bill for him, junk for the trash—when this envelope caught my eye. It was a business envelope, it didn't say 'personal,' it wasn't perfumed, no flowery script or purple ink. I guess it just looked out of place in our usual stuff. So I actually went and heated a teakettle and steamed it open, like in a Hitchcock movie. I was shaking, I felt so scared and guilty."

The letter turned out to be from a woman Mark had been seeing in California. She wanted to visit New York and wondered if Mark would have time to see her, although she said she knew he had a "primary relationship" and wouldn't interfere with that.

" 'Primary relationship'!" Sara sputtered, barely able to contain her fury. "Seven years of supposedly monogamous commitment should rate more than trendy jargon!"

Sara confronted Mark. What really threw her was his reaction to her hurt and anger. He was sorry, he said, to have hurt her, but it was "no big thing. Sex on the road has no meaning, it's just sex." Had Mark explained the encounter away by saying he had been drunk, or lonely, or angry, or somehow out of control, Sara would have been willing to accept and understand. But his assumption that some sex has no meaning was hard for her to digest. "If he could tell me so casually that sex with those other women had no meaning, how does he feel about sex with me? And what did he tell the others about *our* sex life?"

To Sara, and every woman I know, sex *is* a big thing. It's rarely just sex, simply a physical exchange in the dark of the night. Sara simply couldn't understand how Mark could separate his emotions from sex. He, on the other hand, was truly bewildered by Sara's capacity to *impose* emotions on what to him were casual carnal experiences.

APPLES AND ORANGES

cccome said he
umm said she
you're divine said he
you are Mine said she
   e.e. cummings'[1]

In a four-line verse, e.e. cummings put his finger on a central paradox of the eternal male–female dance of desire. Men and women compose love poems to each other, marry until death do them part, find comfort and intimacy with each other in passionate, committed relationships. But despite the great love, need, and sexual desire men have for women and women for men, the most striking disparity I've discovered between them is the dramatically different way men and women view love and sex: women consistently place a higher value on the role of love in a sexual relationship than men.

Logically, you would assume we would pool our human resources: we share the same planet, we are two halves of the same species—genetically, biologically, emotionally, our whole is greater than the sum of our parts. But we seem to regard each other as alien and exotic creatures, alternately loving, fearing, and manipulating each other, rather than dealing with the central paradox of our relationships: men and women need each other, but they often don't operate on the same principles. It's like the grammar school equation where we learned that it was impossible to add oranges and apples.

I think that love is more important to me in a sex relationship than it is to a man; by and large, I need the security of love to feel good about sex. But I think men tend to be more physically oriented—you know, "Go for the gusto."

Linda, 42

Women are more involved with emotions and love and less involved with physical sex. Most men do not seem to show as
much affection as women.

Scott, 29

What role does love play in sex? Is love a biological urge, a
cultural phenomenon? An illusion? Delusion? Of all the influences on a woman's emotional chemistry, the love/sex/love
muddle is one of the most potent. The problem is not love in
and of itself, nor is it sex. It's not even the differences between
men and women. The problem is rather the very different
expectations men and women have about love and sex. "Many
couples in bed together might well be on separate planets for
all the similarity of their perceptions and promises."[2]

SEXUAL MATHEMATICS

I have tried to have several relationships at the same time, but I
can't ever work it out. I always fall in love, get all caught up in
my emotions. Sex isn't what it's hyped up to be. Love can exist
without sex, but sex isn't worth much without love.

Laura, 24

Most women view love as a concomitant part of sex: "love
+ sex = LOVE" is the female equation. No matter how liberated, how sensible we are, if we are female we have been
taught that to separate the role of love from our sexual feelings
leaves us open to the fate of the Bad Girl: ostracism, power-
lessness, loss of personal value. Women turn to the emotion
they can count on to make their sexual lives permissible: love.

Women use sex to get love. Old-fashioned? A silly idea, this
business that we women can't just have sex for the physical
pleasure it gives us? If we can be proud of our other achieve-
ments—our careers, our intellectual abilities—why can't we
simply view coitus as a skill and be proud of our ability to give

and receive pleasure? It's too crass, too blunt, too scary. For us, the equation is sex − love = a rip-off. The veiled contract is very much with us.

Men seem to use love (and words of love) to get sex. The masculine equation of the love/sex puzzle is either sex = sex or sex + love = sex. Men are unencumbered by the complexities of the female equation. They are *not* love junkies. They are *not* brought up to believe that love is the single most important thing in the world, the ultimate goal. So a man tends to integrate his need for love into his overall ambitions and quest for personal satisfaction. And, since he has in fact learned that love may be dangerous, a high-risk emotion that can lead to feelings of entrapment, or of inadequacy through sexual rejection, a man may lessen the potential danger by separating the vulnerable areas of love and sex. It's a way to objectify a woman and thus minimize the possibility of damage. *Unless a relationship is well established, it is more than likely that sex for a man will be unconnected with being in, feeling, or looking for love.*

Something doesn't add up. You're Swept Away by the emotion of the moment. As a thirty-eight-year-old student and part-time secretary described the fantasy, "Carried away by emotion. I think how wonderful it would be to be married, to have his baby, etc. Blinded by love." But the likelihood is he's simply sexually aroused and would, in fact, be appalled by her fantasy.

Love is not a necessary ingredient for a man to enjoy sex. When asked about the connection between the two, only 9 percent of male respondents to a survey said love was necessary to good sex.[3] If it had been reversed, I'll wager 91 percent of women would have said love *was* crucial to good sex.

Women learn that love is selfless, beyond and above sexual desire and satisfaction, on a higher plane than lust. Men can't comprehend why women place lust in a lower category. Love without a dose of lust wouldn't be worth much to a man. This bewildered plaint from a respondent typifies masculine confusion: "The woman I loved wanted a friend, security, reassurance, understanding, someone she enjoyed talking to, someone she could laugh with more than a sexual experience. She wanted everything *but* sex."

Psychologist Beverly Hotchner doesn't think it's necessarily such a bad thing that women value love so highly, as long as they are able to differentiate between love and passion. She attributes the disaccord between men and women partly to social conditioning. "But some of the importance we attach to finding heart's ease is an inner wisdom, an intuitive knowledge that concerns the quality of one's life. We know that sharing love makes living better." Part of the reason we carry the torch, I guess, is that we feel that one man plus one woman *can* equal a stable, satisfying, enriching alliance.

SEX AND LOVE AND POWER

Men learn that control is the essence of manhood: control in the board room, on the playing field, and in the bedroom. While young girls learn docility, young boys are out running and playing, scrapping and building—controlling their environment. For many, this emphasis on control will later translate into anxiety if a relationship is *not* controlled. In this sort of man, his sexuality is governed by specific injunctions: first, not to make a woman pregnant (which assumes that the man must then suffer loss of self-determination by assuming responsibility for her and her child) and, second, not to fall in love, thus losing control of his emotions and becoming vulnerable to rejection:

When a woman can put her claws into you because you love her, you're in trouble. I am very careful about falling in love. It costs too much, emotionally and financially.

Bob, 27

Sentiments similar to Bob's were found by Shere Hite in her study of male sexuality. For example, she discovered that most men had not married the women they most passionately loved because the fear of the irrationality of that kind of emotion made them look for a more "stable" relationship with someone who didn't have the power to dominate them. These men described this maneuver as a "rational decision" and "took pride in having acted wisely, remaining cool and collected, and 'using their heads'—even though they missed their lost love."[4]

It may be, as the writer Shulamith Firestone says, that "men live the female 'emotional' side of their personality on the sly. . . . Love is the underbelly of [male] culture just as love is the weak spot of every man bent on proving his virility in that large male world of 'travel' and 'adventure.' . . . Women have always known how men need love, and how they deny this need."[5]

Our culture has always made it difficult for a man—and imperative for a woman—to admit to love. For men, love takes something away—freedom, property, individuality. But sex enhances a man, repeating and confirming his maleness.

We get stuck in this morass, labeled "old-fashioned," "uptight," or "possessive" if we don't want sex without love. But we don't want to think that a man's need for sex is just "natural impulse." "Romantic passion or passionate romance is what women look for," says Dr. William Fishburn, a psychologist and sex therapist in private practice. "But men aren't as comfortable about romance; typically, they prefer passionate *sex*. Women want to be in love. Even when a man feels in love, and says to the woman he loves, 'I love you,' the meaning of that phrase is interpreted differently by the man and woman. Women look for constant reassurance and say to men, 'Tell me you love me like you mean it.' Then men say, 'I *told* you I love you, I tell you that all the time.' And she still isn't satisfied. *Because for a woman, the 'I love you' legitimizes the sexual involvement.* Now what if a man says, 'I sex you'? Most women probably wouldn't like it at all. But it probably would be more accurate. There is a difference in loving, being in love and making love for women and having sex for men."

In the constant seesaw of the sex/love power struggle, a man can gain dominance over a woman and control over himself by withholding the signs of affection and approval she seeks. Some men continue in a relationship over a long period of time avoiding a declaration of love. They seem to be afraid that "I love you" has some talismanic effect that will grant a woman power.

This lack of ability in men to express, or even feel, loving emotions bothers women. Dr. Beverly Hotchner said of this emotional miscommunication: "Men have real difficulty knowing what women mean by wanting closeness—they don't have the vaguest idea of what that means. They aren't socialized to talk about their feelings; they aren't even socialized to *admit* to feelings, so how can they be expected to talk about love?"

THE PRAGMATIC MALE

If you aren't going all the way, why go at all?

Steve, 36

Men tend to be pragmatic rather than romantic. They are perpetually goal-oriented. Sportsmen say, "A tie is like kissing your sister"; if you don't play to win, why play? This carries over into a man's sex life; he expects experience to have an end goal like a competitive game. "Turn the man loose in a sexually liberated society and tell him he has nothing to do but enjoy himself, and he is likely, instead, to make up some sort of contest, such as how many women he can engage, how many acts he can perform, or how well he can perform them.[6]

It's hard for most women to see sex as notches on a gun or scalps hung from a belt, but it's part and parcel of a man's sex life.

This male pragmatism and gamesmanship extend to his social rituals. Most men see dating or spending the evening out in the company of a woman as a means to an end. What is done during the early part of the evening—a movie, a dinner, the theater—is not as important as what may follow: intercourse.

Researchers have found that not much has changed in the dating game in the last twenty years.[7] Women expect a date to be a beginning, a sociable event, a chance to get to know one another. A date may lead to more, but the "more" it might lead to is perceived by women as romantic rather than sexual. Sex may be a *possibility*, but it depends on the course of the evening and how a woman feels about the man at its end: another gauntlet a man must run. And he, having survived the gauntlet, and having invested both time and money, expects to be repaid with sex.

This was brought home vividly to me during the period when I lived in New York. At a convention of therapists, I met a psychologist from California. He wanted to see a play, and asked me for suggestions. I recommended *Camelot*, and he asked if I'd be interested in going with him, suggesting that we have dinner afterward at a famous New York trattoria. It sounded like fun, and until the tab for dinner arrived, it was.

I knew then that our wires were crossed: not only did he refuse to accept money for my theater ticket, he insisted on picking up the entire, not inconsiderable, check for our dinner. On leaving the restaurant, I flagged a taxi to go home; I sensed that the evening was going to end badly. And when he insisted on "seeing me to my apartment," I turned to him, anxious to be straightforward, and told him I had enjoyed our evening together, and that I was interested in his friendship, but not a sexual relationship.

More than disgruntled or disappointed, he was furious. "Then why did you go out with me?" he snapped.

Our expectations were diametrically different. I had wanted to see the play (Richard Harris was starring, a longtime favorite of mine, and I'd said so). I enjoyed the man's company and respected his work, and the night out had promised to be fun. But now here I was feeling foolish and then angry, pressured into a scenario that had had no place in my plans. I suspect he was feeling as bad as I, and the enjoyment we'd shared during a pleasant evening together dissipated in the dust of the disappearing taxi that bore him away.

Certainly not all men are that single-minded about pursuing sex after a date, but there does seem to be a difference between male and female expectations. It's a mutual ego bruiser: the man feels bad because he's been rejected; the woman feels bad, convinced she was wanted for her sexiness alone, not for the pleasure of her company.

THE "I'LL CALL YOU" SYNDROME

It's lousy to worry and think, "God, I wonder if he'll call? Should I make a date tonight or should I keep myself free? . . ." I could kill myself the times I've waited for the phone to ring and it hasn't rung. I have paid a big price for that, and I don't think I can deal with it any more.

.   *Lauren Bacall*[8]

Nothing symbolizes our love/sex muddle better than the "I'll call you" syndrome. Laura, a top-notch salesperson, told me, "Love, permanent bonds, beautiful life ahead—isn't that what everyone wants? Instead, you wake up in the morning, find the other side of the bed empty and regret starting any relationship at all. He tiptoes out of your life while promising to call you."

It's almost a universal woman's plaint: sex seems to be the end of a relationship, not the beginning, and those three words are the signal it's over. We *do* expect to hear from the man who steals away in the night murmuring, "I'll call you." We get angry because we assume having sex was not as meaningful to the man as it was to us. We are forced to one of two extremes: putting ourselves down, or condemning the man as thoughtless and no good. We sit by the phone, willing it to ring, treating it as a lifeline to love. My trick to will a call was to stare at the phone and send out waves via ESP: "Pick up the receiver . . . dial my number . . . ask me out." When totally desperate, I would even lift the receiver and scream into the buzzing emptiness, "CALL ME!"

Psychologist Penelope Russianoff comments on the unrealistic rules a woman may have for the proper progression of a relationship: " 'He shouldn't have dropped me. It's not morally right.' That reaction has to do with socialization, not sexual desire. I say it's fine for a woman to go ahead and have sex but she shouldn't expect the man to call her the next day." [9]

And therapist Natalie Mackler is refreshlingly blunt: "Men don't call women as they promised because they don't want to." Linda Blocki, editor of *Single Scene*, attributes the misconstruction to "the problem of different dialects, a conflicting approach to language. Perhaps men don't realize it when they speak with a forked tongue, but women, who are more literal-minded according to communication researchers, take their words seriously. Since women, in general, actually mean what they say, they expect that men do too. 'I'll call you tomorrow' means to a woman that she'll hear from you the very next day, whereas men tend to fling such lines around more carelessly. Translation: 'I'll call you sometime—when I feel like it, next week, or when the Taj Mahal becomes a Safeway.' " [10] And Joel, a forty-year-old anthropologist, spoke to the point: "Yeah, I've told women I'd call them when I had no intention of ever speaking to them again. It seemed only polite, a way of easing out the door without a scene. It seemed to be what they expected in return for sex."

Men fail to recognize that seduction to a woman is not only a step on the way to an erotic encounter but a confirmation that the encounter is special. And women don't realize that men aren't aware of this. "I don't understand it," said Tom, a twenty-four-year-old business-machine salesman. "Women make such a damned big issue out of everything I say. They act like I tried to fool them by flirting with them, but they flirt like crazy, drape themselves all over me, and have a great time having sex. The next morning they act like I'm some sort of monster because I don't necessarily want them for my best friends. They accuse me—'You said,' 'You did.' It's too bad they couldn't just enjoy what we had." And why not? Because women need to believe that sex isn't just a transitory physical thing. So they gild the lily.

THE VANISHING MAN

We saw each other every night for six weeks. I was really swept off my feet and thinking about asking him to move in. Without any warning, he stopped calling and was vague and distant when I called him. Finally, I demanded to discuss what was going on. And he said, "There's nothing to talk about. I just don't think we should be seeing so much of each other."

Janet, 33

Not only do they not call, men walk out. I hear it again and again. Women are bewildered by the way men seem to exit casually after months of intimacy. "Why," they ask, "don't men want to have real and solid relationships?" Sometimes it seems like a cruel twist on the standard Hollywood plot: woman meets man, woman gets man, woman loses man. And that makes us feel "set up, sucked in, used, abused, screwed, blued and tattooed," as one verbal and embittered woman put it.

Shirley has a responsible position with a state government office dealing with women's issues. She is organized in her career and in her life, not a woman to jump without looking carefully first. Hardly a candidate for being Swept Away.

She met Daniel at a fund-raising event, and after a few

lunches they went out on a "real" date. One date led to another, and after several months they became a "couple." They
spent most week nights and every weekend together. Visits to
respective parents' homes followed, and the future looked, as
Shirley said, "positively rosy."

Then came Black Friday: Shirley called Daniel at work to
check on weekend plans. They'd been invited to a Sunday
picnic in the mountains; did he want to go? Daniel was distant,
noncommittal . . . said he'd get back to her. Saturday night he
was unable to tell her yes or no; after spending the night, he
left saying he didn't think he'd go, but that she should.

Although they'd been in touch every day for months, their
next conversation was ten days later when Shirley finally
reached him on the phone at work. After hemming and haw-
ing, Daniel told her they should stop seeing each other so
much and begin to date others. As a beginning, he was leaving
the next day for a two-week trip to Europe, but they would
"get together when he returned."

They never did. He never communicated with her again—
"not even a lousy postcard."

"But wasn't there a teeny clue?" I asked her. "A hint, or
some change in his behavior that perplexed you?"

"No," Shirley said. "I swear it all looked hunky-dory."

I was determined to get to the root of this, so I gave her a
virtual third degree, and at last the break began to make sense.
She'd always wanted children; he was recently divorced, had
two children of his own, and was paying child support—quite
a hefty sum, in fact. He was perfectly willing to commit himself to a stable and loving relationship with Shirley, but he was
absolutely not in the market for a second family. Shirley
blithely ignored his very real bias: "I figured he'd grow into
wanting children with me. And the picnic in the mountains
was going to be so special. My sister was bringing her two
kids. I thought he'd see how wonderful I was with children,
and how wonderful children are, and we'd go home that night
and make love—maybe even conceive a baby then and there."

Instead, Daniel bolted. Shirley had ignored the signals he'd given her throughout their relationship in favor of a fantasy of her own—a fantasy that defined sex as love and marriage and family. In order to have her version of love, she kidded herself, feeling that with just one more effort, he'd come around. She hyped his attributes and diminished what for her were his shortcomings—his refusal to have children. She concentrated on the rapture they felt together, and let herself be blind to what was really going on.

In case after case, when women announce their bewilderment at the end of a long-term relationship, I've discovered that their men didn't lie to them—they'd deluded themselves. All too often we don't take a good honest look at what we have, and so we're shocked when our rose-colored glasses get shattered.

FANCY FRENCH RESTAURANTS

I've discovered that an unexpected visit to a fancy French restaurant all too often means the end of an affair, especially if we've been having trouble.

Mary Lou, 34

I had to laugh at Mary Lou's wisecrack, but my laughter had a rueful ring. When a man wants to make a "clean break" with a woman (as opposed to simply disappearing), it *is* often standard practice for him to invite her out to dinner at a quiet, expensive restaurant in order to break the news. The woman is then constrained by the public nature of the place from making a scene, and the man assuages his conscience by paying for an expensive, expiating last supper.

I asked Dr. Hotchner why in fact it seemed that men don't act, well, more honorably. Why can't they just be more direct, talk about what they want; why are they so sly?

"Men are not trained to talk about their feelings," she answered. "That makes it doubly hard to talk about something so close to the bone as a relationship. Ending a love affair is hard for anyone, but men have more trouble expressing the reasons than women.

"Women want and need closure. All of our fairytales have endings, we want our real-life stories to be as neat and tidy. Even if the ending is unhappy, we want a finale. We've learned from talking among ourselves that verbalizing a problem helps to sort it out, make it less painful.

"If men can't discuss their simplest emotions, imagine how hard it is to discuss complex ones, guilt-inducing ones, ones that cause injury to another. Many men even undergo physiological changes when forced to 'talk about it.' Their pulse rates and heartbeats soar; they sweat. It seems to them that the easiest way to be kind—and at the same time avoid pain —is to *act* rather than linger endlessly over discussions of feelings they would much rather not feel, much less talk about."

SEX MAKES THE WORLD GO ROUND

"Love makes the world go round," goes the old adage, but the truth is that *sex* ensures that the species continues so that it can tangle with emotional concepts like love. Without love the world would be a pretty bleak place, but without sex, we'd die out in a generation. And one guarantee that this won't happen is the elemental force that sexual attraction has, the magnetism of purely physical response to physical stimuli; one woman I interviewed labeled its effect the "post-orgasmic glow," that walking-on-air feeling of satisfaction and contentment with which a good sexual experience leaves us.

Masters and Johnson's pioneering studies of sexual response gave us a schematic understanding of the way the body works and pointed out the physiological universality of sexual feelings and reactions.[11] The vendors of romance clearly understand how biological imperatives are translated into warm and passionate reactions to another person. Take, for instance, our romance heroine's response when she meets the handsome heir: "Sabretta's heart began to hammer, as if the entire crew of the building under construction at 57th Street and Madison Avenue was working inside her . . . her pulse began to race, as if it were a marathon runner gone amok. Her stomach somersaulted, as if members of Ringling Brothers were rehearsing within her. For a fleeting moment she thought she might faint." [12] While Sabretta's reaction *is* a bit extreme for most of us, we are all creatures of sexual desires and the physiological responses these needs trigger.

Our whole body is biologically geared toward sex and orgasm. And interestingly, men's and women's sexual biology is more similar than different. When we are attracted to someone, our hypothalamus—that bundle of tissue at the base of our brain—acting through the long-distance messenger of the pituitary gland, modulates our blood pressure, temperature, and breathing rate, and heightens our sexual appetite. [13] Somewhere in the wash of hormones and the complex brain-talk of the messenger chemicals, a wordless decision is made that intercourse is the next event and nerve impulses race back and upward, to spine, to brain, to hypothalamus. Our muscles stiffen, heart beats fast, pupils dilate. A rise in circulating estrogen makes the vagina moist. The erectile tissues of the man's penis are suffused with blood, calling up testosterone and an accelerated sperm production: a tightness is felt in his loins. Blood rushes to her vagina leading to moisture seeping across its lining; the clitoris is enlarging, breasts enlarge, the aureoles surrounding the nipples swell. The tissues of his penis fill up with more blood, the testes rise up closer to the body and balloon up half again their usual size.

Arousal gets more intense, and the control of the reasoning forebrain switches over to the control of the lower brain and the autonomic nervous system. The chest becomes flushed with a pale red, body heat rises, nipples become erect, breath comes shorter and faster. Slowly the sympathetic nervous tension builds to a higher pitch. Muscles contract rhythmically. The uterus rises, the clitoris withdraws. The tension becomes intense. The adrenal glands are pumping out testosterone in a mix of other hormones, making her clitoris more sensitive and giving him an extra urgency, centered on the reflex arc that governs his erection from nerve centers at the base of the spine. The muscles of his penis contract, he tenses and, beyond his control, nerve impulses race toward his brain. With a great exhalation of air he climaxes and ejaculates a stream of semen. Contractions ripple along the walls of her vagina, and the uterus contracts. A new hormone, oxytocin, releases from her pituitary. Her skin slightly darkens, the muscles surrounding the vagina contract rhythmically every eight-tenths of a second, and past the point of no return: she plummets into relief. The uterus dips down into a cuplike widening in the upper vagina (the better for sperm to enter the womb). Then, heartbeat slows, blood pressure drops, and where before there was tension, there is now a drift into calmness.

While each of us describes "orgasm" differently, and reaches it through different means of stimulation, there are measurable body responses that occur. That feeling you get of "electrical" attraction is reflected in actual brain wave activity; "falling head over heels in love" is a verbalization of these complex hormonal changes.

Dr. Michael R. Liebowitz, a psychiatrist at Columbia University, suggests that there are in fact two separate chemical changes that occur in the human body, reflecting the difference between sexual attraction and love attachment. Sexual attraction has intercourse as its immediate goal; love concerns the feelings one has for another person beyond simple physical satisfaction.

Dr. Liebowitz theorizes that when people experience what is commonly recognized as "falling in love," a chemical chain reaction is triggered by the *appearance* of a person who fits an unconscious image of a desirable mate: his hair, eyes, the way

he laughs or smokes his cigarette, or any of a million characteristics that signal your ideal. The brain becomes "a bath of
dopamine and norepinephrine," two of the more than thirty
chemical substances that are neurotransmitters—messengers
that bridge the gaps or synapses between the body's millions
of nerve cells.

Exactly how this brain chemistry translates into "I am in
love" is little understood, but the physical reactions are familiar: the heart beats harder, the breath comes faster, the face
flushes, and we feel excited, happy, and full of pleasurable
anticipation. Dr. Liebowitz believes that these neurochemical
fluctuations involve a naturally occurring amphetamine substance and form a pathway somewhat analogous to electrical
currents wired into machines. Researchers hypothesize that
this chemical activity affects the threshold of the brain's pleasure center, which accounts for the enjoyable sensations we
feel when we're with a person who attracts us. These romantic
responses seem to be one of the most powerful activators of
our pleasure centers, giving lovers that "transcendent feeling,
a feeling beyond time, space and your own body."

But alas, these peak love experiences, these episodes of
being emotionally swept away, cannot last. In the natural process of being around the other person, the thrill of first attraction is dispelled. The initial romantic sensation either dissolves
or evolves into a state that Dr. Liebowitz identifies as attachment—that sturdy day-in, day-out intimacy that is the goal
most women seek in a committed relationship. Scottie, a fea-
ture writer for a major newspaper in her mid-thirties, described the unfolding of her six-year romance: "I loved the
beginning of my love affair with David when sex was unbe-
lievably terrific and I was horny for him day and night. The
fire's died down to a nice glowing ember, constant but not
showy. I think the thing that symbolizes the comfortableness
of our relationship is this image I have of the two of us on a
cold winter's night snuggled up together in bed—*reading!*"

Scottie's affair traveled the road from Swept Away to close
attachment: a warm, calming emotion, often associated with

the lessening of anxiety, which involves another set of chemical alterations in the body. Rather than amphetamine-like substances, the brain produces a group of soothing narcotics called endorphins, which are secreted when a person is in a comfortable social situation.

Dr. Liebowitz theorizes that the differing states of attraction and attachment may even have had evolutionary value. "A prerequisite for our species to survive was that, first, adults would be attracted to one another to mate, and second, that the offspring would be protected so they can survive their long period of helplessness. Attachment not only tied mothers and infants together for long periods of time but also kept the fathers involved." [14]

A mother/wife/secretary/graduate student of forty (she specified the order on her questionnaire) said, "When I was sixteen, I fell deeply 'in love.' I was totally involved in our magical dating experiences. I was also much more interested in him than in myself; you might say I lost myself in him. I felt the same way about my husband when I met him at nineteen. We've been married for twenty years now and have three children. I'm still in love with him, but in a different way."

But when you're suffering from the no-phone-call syndrome, it's cold comfort to know you may be, among other things, the victim of your own biology. Where we seem to have gone astray is in the importance our culture puts on the more electrical emotion—attraction—which becomes the measure of our love. We have trouble valuing the calm and settled-in nature of an attachment relationship. We keep seeking to recapture the thrills we have learned to (mis)identify as love.

WORDPLAY

Describing the experience of coitus can be very telling. "Having sex" may, for a man, describe years of physical pleasure and intimacy with one woman or minutes of orgasmic release with a series of near-strangers. While a woman may say "making love" to describe sexual intercourse—whether it was a hurried encounter or a passionate exchange within a stable relationship—she is describing *not* the physical act but what she feels or hopes the emotions were. Most men would choke at describing sexual intercourse with someone to whom they are not solidly committed as "making love."

In fact, men use a larger number of synonyms for sexual intercourse than women. At the workshops on human sexuality I conducted, my colleague Paul Dearth and I developed an exercise that underlines the sex/love muddle semantically. We asked people to list the words they felt best described coitus. The women's first choice was "making love"; the men's, "sex" or "having sex." "Fuck" was the word most disliked by women, but men had a hard time isolating a word that bothered them.

These semantic preferences extend into literature and the way male and female novelists treat sex and love. Ann Barr Snitow found that male novelists tend either to view sex as "animalistic" or use it as a symbol of "failed transcendence." Snitow says, "In a straight line of descent from F. Scott Fitzgerald to Philip Roth and Saul Bellow, male novelists have been using sexual disappointments to symbolize deceleration in the forward thrust of life in general. This group continues to show men seducing, betraying, possessing, and being bored by their possession, moving on to the next woman while obsessing continuously about that one in a million who cannot be bought or possessed, who has betrayed them and driven them out of the Garden of Eden.

"Women are perhaps lucky that their real sexuality is so secondary an issue that no such monolithic importance has been ascribed to it." [15]

For women novelists sexual performance is not the measure of *femaleness*. Success in romance *is*—as the enormous popularity of romance fiction testifies. In literature getting a man is considered more of a women's testing ground than sexual performance. And although literature doesn't have to mirror life, in these instances the reflections seem to be fairly true to the love/sex dichotomy. Dorothy Parker, that cynical limner of the male/female dance, observed:

> Man delights in novelty.
> Love is woman's moon and sun;
> Man has other forms of fun.
> Woman lives but in her lord;
> Count to ten, and man is bored.
> With this the gist and sum of it,
> What earthly good can come of it?[16]

SURVEYS AND STATISTICS

Instinct isn't the only thing that informs us that there is a vast difference between men and women—that we're in separate worlds concerning sex and love. Where there is controversy, there are studies, and when I took a look at the information that sociologists, psychologists, anthropologists, and other professionals had compiled, I found some consistent information.

• One study of reasons for first intercourse broke down the sex/love division like this: 46 percent of men said they had sex for the first time because of appetite or desire, while only 16 percent of the females agreed. But 42 percent of women respondents said they had sex for the first time because they were in love, as compared to 10 percent of males.[17]

• In a study of 1,079 college students, researchers discovered that women thought about romance more than males did: "Sociologically, this phenomenon is attributed to a directedness in the females' romantic orientation for which there appears to be no male counterpart."[18]

- Researchers looking for social influences on romantic love queries 243 males and females. Their findings? Women were more likely to have experienced "romantic attraction" than men, but men were more idealistic about romance. The researchers discovered more differences between men and women over romantic love than similarities.[19]

- Differences in expectations of love and sex may be linked to socioeconomic status as well as gender. The double standard is stronger in the blue-collar economic strata, and women who have premarital sex are more likely to be considered "cheap" and "dirty" by both men and women. Women in this group seemed to consider sex a means of pleasing their man; they professed more interest in romance than in sex.[20]

- Naomi B. McCormick discovered in a survey of 120 male and 109 female unmarried students that "both traditional and profeminist students continue to expect a sexual dating script in which the male attempts to gain access to the female's body and the female either passively accepts the male's advances or actively blocks his efforts. . . . It is quite possible . . . that many sex differences in the use of power are a function of differences in the *goal* sought."[21]

Psychologist Carol Robert asked her students at San Diego Mesa College to list problems they had with any aspect of sexual functioning—psychological, physiological, or social. The responses:

WOMEN'S PROBLEMS
Fear of pregnancy
Being rejected for refusing to have sex

Loss of self-respect
Sexual inadequacy—inability to be orgasmic or satisfy
   partner
Pressure to have sex
Fear of being conquered and left

MEN'S PROBLEMS
Passive women
Aggressive women
Excessively modest women
Women who tease sexually or manipulate
Women who are closed to various sexual experiences
Having to always be on the hunt for a woman
Necessity to declare love, even when untrue
Being expected to know all about sex[22]

What all this means is that when it comes to sexual concerns,
women talk about insecurity, guilt, and fears. But men objectify their sexual partners and talk about the mechanics. Oddly
—and perhaps tellingly—while women worry about their own
emotional needs, neither sex seems to expend much concern
on men's emotions.

LOVE IS STRANGE

"Love," wailed Mickey and Sylvia in the old Motown hit,
"looove is strange." Maybe the definitions—and there are almost as many as there are people—are at fault. If you think
the sex/love muddle is confusing, you're in good company.
Even the experts can't agree. Theories range from pole to pole.
   Some people think every physical act of an intimate nature,
even hugging, between adults is erotically tinged. Joyce, a
woman in her early fifties, typified this point of view: "*Everything* we do is really sexual. Friends, male or female, would
never bother with a friendship if there wasn't a sexual attrac-

tion in the first place. That doesn't mean they will have sex, or even recognize the attraction, but it exists." Dr. David Shope agrees. "Love stems from the sensuous need to be near others, to be touched and to experience this touch as psychologically satisfying. Love grows out of a biological need, sensuousness, and is differentiated in awareness from sexuality because of social conditioning." [23] And Freud felt love was simply the way we divert our basic biological urge in a socially acceptable way.

Sociologist Ira Reiss sees love not as physical in origin, but rather as a process of rapport, self-revelation, and mutual dependency, followed by personality-need fulfillment. [24] Researcher Robert Hazo found, in analyzing love in literature, that most authors agree that love is a tendency to action, a desire to be with the beloved in a "union of wholeness." [25] Stendhal penned an early description of the Swept Away phenonemon when he wrote that we fall in love "with an imaginary person whom we invent to fulfill all our needs, desires and wishes." [26]

Love and sex may be inherently in conflict: sex is, by its nature, an act that requires people to be in a close merger. "Love" according to philosopher Robert Soloman, "is a taut line of opposed desires between the ideal of an eternal merger of souls and our cultivated urge to prove ourselves as free and autonomous individuals." [27] Finding a balance on that tightrope between self and other while trying to integrate the roles of love and sex requires more skill than most of us, male or female, can muster.

Perhaps Professor Soloman's argument for the particularity of each experience is the closest we can come to defining love: "Love is, in a phrase, an emotion through which we create for ourselves a little world—the love-world—in which we play the roles of lovers and create ourselves as well." [28] As Charlie Brown, that "Peanuts" philosopher, advises, "I can recommend a book, or a painting, or a song, or a poem, but I can't explain love . . . You not only can't explain love . . . actually, you can't even talk about it." [29]

However, no matter how you struggle to define it, love isn't the sole prerogative of women. The difference in the way men and women balance the roles of love and sex doesn't mean that men don't feel love or women sexual desire. Both men and women find that love is deeper and more exciting when it's enhanced by sexual chemistry. I've been told by my husband that I love him because of lust. I can't deny it; I can't separate love from sexual compatibility.

But women get caught up in the love/sex muddle because we feel, or think we feel, every sexual encounter is really potentially a love encounter, while men don't feel that same way. When we can really face up to the difference, without fault-finding or rancor, we will have eliminated a potent element in the tension and battle fatigue that exist between the sexes. But "when" may be a long way off, and we have to live in the present in our climate of confusion. Dr. Fishburn put it succinctly: "Women get Swept Away. Men get Sexed Away."

4

STILL GOOD GIRLS AFTER ALL THESE YEARS

SOCIAL CONTROL

I was brought up to be a Good Girl. I was taught never to cause anger, disgust, disappointment or inconvenience. I learned to try and please everyone.

Anonymous, 45

This terse comment in a batch of responses to my questionnaire gave me an uncomfortable jolt of recognition. In the bare economy of those lines, I recognized the narrowness and confinement of generations of women's lives, circumscribed by the amorphous and insidious credo of the Good Girl.

One aspect of who we are is encoded in the messages we receive about who we *should* be. We learn that certain behavior is rewarded, other behavior punished. If we learn not to squander our sexual goods on unworthy males, we also know that to be eligible for the attention of the worthy ones, we must follow certain rules and regulations. We must be worthy ourselves: Good Girls. The term has endless connotations: chaste, kind, sweet, virtuous, cheerful, coy, and above all, *above reproach*. We learn this from the way society regulates our behavior, setting up standards of female decorum, using a form of social control that sociologist Greer Litton Fox identifies as "normative restrictions."[1]

Normative restrictions as a social control work because the culture as a whole shares the same values, the same "norms." Thus the whole culture is enlisted to preserve the norms: if a member deviates, he or she becomes a pariah. When the norm is that women's behavior should conform to the social ideal of a "lady," her failure to adhere to this prescription means that it is *her* fault that she is an outcast, not society's fault for having an inflexible or untenable norm. She is thus due any consequences that befall her: ostracism, loss of value as a person, even, in certain societies, public humiliation and death by stoning. It seems an extreme fate for a Bad Girl, doesn't it?

One of the most pervasive norms of our culture is sexual restraint: "A girl is in a delicate position. She is told to appear and act 'sexy' in order to attract as many boys and have as many dates as possible. . . . But at the same time she must hold the line of propriety, because otherwise she risks losing her 'good girl' status and, consequently, her prestige."[2] Only if a woman is madly in love, swept off her feet, can she still claim any vestige of her Good Girl status. A woman "in love" is released from the burden of being good so that she can be erotic. She's a nonsexual being who lapsed temporarily into sexuality. She is "overcome" by passion. Sex is something that happens *to* her. Barbara, twenty-seven, explained how she gave herself permission to be sexual. "I shouldn't admit this, but I can't have sex unless the man I'm with is really persuasive and takes a firm hold of the situation. I'm not talking about rape or anything like that, but he can't just let me beg off too eagerly. He has to sweep me off my feet or I can't enjoy it."

If she initiated a sexual encounter, Barbara feels that she would lose the temporary suspension of the rules of proper behavior that passion allows, leaving her susceptible to condemnation and unworthy of masculine attention. Dr. Karen Cantrell, an anthropologist studying women and power, defines this sexual side-stepping as an aligning action, as the way a woman attempts to resolve the conflict between her pesonal desire and society's prohibitions. "A woman may account for her sexual behavior by disclaiming responsibility for her actions. She can't be blamed for breaking the rules about sex if *she wasn't in control.* Allowing herself to be overcome by a skillful lover puts the responsibility on the man for her breech." Her need, sexual fulfillment, has been neatly aligned with society's—that she remain nonsexual. She wasn't sexual; the *man* was.

In refusing to acknowledge and deal with her needs, a woman relies on a man's permission, via seduction, to be erotic. The "terrible" power of a woman's sexuality—that eternal power that binds men to women—is constrained when she hands responsibility for it over to a man. A Good Girl, sexual only in male-approved circumstances, is a controlled and dependent woman, relieved of adulthood. Her sexual passivity affects her life as well as her libido. Unable to stand on her own two feet, she must resort to attempting to bind a man to her in the veiled contract.

MAKING "GOOD"

When I was growing up, the topic of sex was "hush-hush." It was never talked about in my family. I regret that it was not. I think I would be a different human being today if we could have talked about it. I didn't know as a child that sex was for making babies; I learned from my peers that it was something dirty to do.

Anonymous, 21

How do you create a Good Girl? It starts in childhood. Society still doesn't say to girls, "Sex is wonderful. It feels physically pleasurable; it can make you feel emotionally satisfied and good about yourself. There are no rules except (1) Don't

get pregnant unless you plan to; (2) Don't get a sexually transmitted disease; and (3) Don't be exploitative." Nowhere is it
clearly stated to a young woman that sex is a normal and
natural part of life experience.

> I was taught that sex was the most beautiful thing *if two people
> were in love.* I always convince myself, if only momentarily, that
> I am in love.
>
> *N.N., 27*

There are rules, and we learn the lessons well. Sex is meaningful *only* with the right man, *only* in a proper relationship
(usually marriage). If the rules aren't spoken aloud, an uncomfortable silence delivers the message.

According to Masters and Johnson, "During her formative
years the female dissembles much of her developing sexuality
in response to social requirements. . . . Instead of being
taught or allowed to value her sexual feelings in anticipation
of appropriate and meaningful opportunity for expression,
thereby developing a realistic social value system, she must
attempt to repress or remove them from their natural context
of environmental stimulation."[3] The most pervasive message
young women get is *don't* if you want to be loved and respected. As one twenty-two-year-old woman said, "Females
have rights in sex and life but it's not necessarily *ladylike* to
practice them."

We hear this message at the most unlikely times—pulling
the covers back on the bed in anticipation of making love in
the middle of the afternoon, glancing in the mirror and seeing
yourself taking his shirt off. Voices out of the past, the whispering of the mind combined with the gut feeling that you're
doing something just not "right," something an authentic
Good Girl would never do.

Our society has institutionalized the negative messages that
we give our young girls, and still attempts to legislate proper
behavior. Senator Jeremiah Denton and like-minded congres-

sional leaders succeeded in getting passed the "Chastity Bill" of 1981. It was purportedly intended to help combat the staggering number of teenage pregnancies—about one million a year. It appropriated money for projects helping teenage *girls* to say no to sexual intercourse. Not one penny was budgeted to providing birth control information: it was a $30 million "Hold the Hymen" campaign, designed to pressure young women to learn to be "good."

Marjory Mecklenberg, who directed the Adolescent Family Life Program of the Department of Health and Human Services, tried to get legislation passed that would force family planning officials to notify the parents of teens served (read teenager girls here: they are 33 percent of the clientele at family planning clinics). She said she had no illusions about getting teenagers to give up sex, but she felt that counselors should try to dissuade them before they start.

There has been a flurry of sex-education material directed at the "problem." Government posters list dire consequences to teenagers having sex. All the pamphlets advise young *women* to say no under the guise of self-determination. But the answer in the pamphlets, unlike in real life, is never "yes" to sex, nor does the question—to have sex or withhold it—ever seem to be directed at the boy. In a book for teenagers on sex and love, author Ray E. Short listed twenty-five arguments for and *thirty-four* against premarital sex, mostly directed to girls. And a book publisher's recent ad in the *New York Times* trumpeted, "Premarital sex. It's sweeping America because of today's records, movies, magazines and TV. Here are the facts you must know to get your *daughter* safely through dangerous years." The ad is for *Heartbreak U.S.A.*, which promises to "give your *daughter* the knowledge and ability to resist the incredible pressure being placed on her. . . . This book will help any young girl live up to the standards of conduct which were normal and expected, until recently." (Emphasis added.) It's a manual for becoming a Good Girl, a $12.95 solution to the "misery" and "heartbreak"of premarital sex.[4]

Teaching a young girl to be uncomfortable about her sexuality extends to her feelings about her body. Natural functions become occasions for embarrassment; attitudes that seem appropriate to the dark ages are all too apparent today. In a 1981 research report of the Tampax company based on a survey of 1,000 people, almost two-thirds (66 percent) felt that menstruation should not be discussed in the office or socially. One-quarter of the respondents felt it was an unacceptable topic for the family at home; one-third felt that even in her own home, a woman should conceal the fact that she was having her period. The most startling and dismaying attitude was that 12 percent of male respondents felt that women should make every effort to avoid contact with other people while menstruating, and 5 percent of the women—*very* Good Girls—agreed![5]

In my own "liberated" household I was brought up short when I asked my seventeen-year-old stepdaughter to buy tampons, a supply for herself, her sister, and me. She blushed and said, "I'll buy yours, but that's all for now. Lisa can get her own, and I'll buy mine when I go to the store again."

I was surprised. "What is this about? Are you feeling embarrassed?"

"I know I shouldn't be, but there are lots of guys from school who work there and I don't want to show up with a basket full of Tampax at the check-out counter."

I remembered the feeling from thirty years ago; I had hoped that I could spare my children, but even if we manage the miracle of raising a daughter who is not ashamed of her normal functions we cannot control the influence of her classmates, friends, and the boys at the check-out counter.

Columnist and moral arbiter Abigail Van Buren is certainly one of the most widely read authorities on proper behavior. Readers write her constantly about their concerns with virginity and premarital sex. Not long ago a reader asked her to repeat the advice to girls that she issued years ago:

Girls need to "prove their love" through illicit sex relations like a moose needs a hat rack.

Why not prove your love by sticking your head in the oven and turning on the gas, or playing leap-frog out in the traffic? It's about as safe.

Any fellow who asks you to "prove your love" is trying to take you for the biggest, most gullible fool who ever walked. That proving bit is one of the oldest and rottenest lines ever invented!

Does he love you? Someone who loves you wants whatever is best for you. He wants you to:

Commit an immoral act.

Surrender your virtue.

Throw away your self-respect.

Risk the loss of your precious reputation.

And risk getting into trouble.

Does that sound as if he wants what's best for you? He wants what's best for him . . . he wants a thrill he can brag about at your expense.

Love? A boy who loves a girl would sooner cut off his right arm than hurt her. If you want my opinion, this self-serving so-and-so has already proved that he doesn't love you. The aftermaths of "proofs" of this kind always find Don Juan tiring of his sport. That's when he drops you, picks up his line and goes casting elsewhere for bigger, equally silly fish.[6]

Even if unintended by "Dear Abby," untold numbers of young girls may have gotten the idea from this column that premarital sex is dangerous, morally wrong, and liable to punishment. Now, in addition to the other messages, we have the current public schools' education programs on AIDS. Well intended and urgently needed as these efforts are, the majority are simply warmed-over versions of the "Just say no" (to premarital sex) campaigns focused on girls.

If one million teenaged girls get pregnant every year, that means, as a recent Planned Parenthood public service announcement pointed out, one million teenaged boys were fathers. In an ostrich-like and time-honored fashion, our society virtually ignores male involvement, even to a degree condoning it. We concentrate our prohibitive energy on the female, so that her entry into the sexual world is guilt-laden and fearful. We know, statistically, that almost every young woman in this country will have had sex by the age of nineteen, but because of our societal fear of promiscuity, we choose not to inform our daughters of the real benefits of intercourse—closer relationship, a sense of intimacy, physical release. Even when we are sincerely and justifiably concerned that teens are having sex before they are emotionally and physically ready, and feel that peer pressure needs counterbalancing, we add to the problem if we don't acknowledge that there are positive aspects of sex. Another generation of girls is growing up right now, ashamed and misinformed, and ripe to fall victim to their own ambivalence.

REFLECTED IMAGES

I don't remember ever really hearing about being a good girl *per se*. But I learned about what to do and what not to do about sex from my mother although she never said anything specific. I don't remember even one conversation, but I understand exactly what is acceptable to her and what isn't.

Katie, 21

In my reflection in the mirror, I catch glimpses of my mother —her eye shape, the same tilt of the head; her hair springy and curly, slightly graying in the same streak as hers. And gazing at my daughter, I see myself at twenty-five: slim, brown-eyed, with the same wide smile. I know these physical resemblances are simply outward but they are the visible signs reflecting an invisible but equally strong heritage of attitudes. Virginia Woolf knew. "We think back through our mothers if we are women," she said. And project forward onto our daughters, she might have added. "A mother does not merely pass on the messages of her culture; she also passes on her responses to the messages she received from *her* mother. Thus every transaction between mother and daughter in a sense is a transaction among three generations."[7] Daughters, because they are the female descendants of the female, are the primary heirs of a mother's psyche.

Yet nothing differentiates the behavior of women today from yesteryear as clearly as the fact that most women have had sexual intercourse with more than one man. The tradition of sex with one man throughout a lifetime, a custom practiced almost universally by our grandmothers and widely by our mothers, seems on the verge of disappearing. In a survey of 106,000 readers, *Cosmopolitan* magazine reported that 68 percent had more than one lover.[8]

And yet, and yet . . . The women who were brought up in the fifties are raising the women of the eighties. For all of the movements and social change over the last few decades, the fact of the matter is that daughters are raised pretty much as they always have been. Childhood training and cultural conditioning to be dependent on a man for support and status are well documented.[9] Women still suffer from passivity, a desire to be sheltered and protected from the male world of competition. We find it difficult to be sexually assertive, to develop an individual sense of worth, and to feel self-confident because many of us are still taught to believe in the superiority of the male sex. Try as we might, we can't cut loose from the ties that bind us to a world of love and sex formed in the generations before us.

Researcher Doris Block looked at the messages that the generation of women who came of age sexually in the 1960s hand on to their daughters. These women, now in their middle thirties, were the first to be the beneficiaries of the sexual revolution. They are all in agreement that they suffered from inadequate sexual knowledge, and to a woman they were concerned that their daughters be spared. But, unable to act on their convictions, they glossed over topics or put off the "talk." "I don't think she's interested yet" was a common excuse. The information that *was* conveyed was limited. These mothers were able to discuss the biology of pregnancy: spermatazoa and egg converging are remote enough not to be threatening. But the father's role, and the emotional force and the physical pleasure of intercourse, were left largely unexplained. These supposedly modern women said the same thing old-fashioned mothers did about sex: nothing much.[10]

"I'm nothing like my mother" was repeated to me by everyone from high school students to mature women with established careers. But the more I examined attitudes and behavior, the more I ran across emotional baggage as outdated as great-grandmother's steamer trunk.

"Times are different," we explain patiently (and patronizingly?) to our mothers. But isn't there a slight prickliness, a defensive feeling because we know we are still being judged —and judging ourselves—through our mothers' eyes? "When my mother comes to town to visit me, I become a whirlwind of activity to hide any evidence of sleeping around. It's insane: I hide my diaphragm and his shaving cream, throw away stray toothbrushes. I even launder *all* the sheets, like she was going to give me some kind of bed check for stray pubes or stains. I know it's silly, but I can't be straightforward and stand up for my own way of life. After all, I'm a grown woman. I'm thirty years old. But I just can't disappoint her," said a Good Girl. And Ruth, thirty-three, told me about her grandmother's influence: "Every time I get a letter from her—she's eighty years old—she ends with, 'Be a good girl.' I asked her what she meant. 'You *know*,' she answered. Once I asked her to spell out what being a good girl means. She hedged; all she could get out was that it had to do with men, and that I really *do* know what she's talking about. She drives me crazy when she does this."

I discovered an interesting phenomenon dealing with maternal messages when I was in the Dominican Republic with my then-husband. It was the early 1960s, I was in my late twenties, and he was a staff member of the Peace Corps. I went along. Status: wife, mother, "helpmate." It was an eye-opening trip for me: the culture of the Dominicans was no more alien to me than the company of the young women, Peace Corps volunteers, who became my friends and confidantes.

At home, I had lived in a neighborhood of young families like my own. I knew most of the women on the block, we exchanged baby-sitters and had coffee klatches regularly, but our conversation was guarded and our actual level of communication about our lives and hopes and dreams was very low. The women in the Peace Corps were a new breed: slightly younger than I, already influenced by the stirrings of the women's liberation movement and the sexual revolution, they and not the natives were the true exotics to me. My obvious experience in family matters (four children) and my apparent maturity made me a sort of mater familias for the group. What an education; those women talked about *everything*—orgasms, being horny, who was a great lover, who was a terrible lover.

Most of the women had responded to pressure from their mothers about being "good" and "nice" with mild rebellion but ultimate compliance. But, transported to a foreign clime out of striking distance of home and thus freed from the specter of maternal disapproval, and further absolved from social condemnation by an exotic setting where hometown values no longer held, these women gave themselves permission to be sexual.

How lucky they were, I would think, as they dashed off to work in Peace Corps jeeps. Lucky, lucky not to be stuck with the 1950s vision of a woman. These young women looked so free and acted so casual. At first. But as time—and the telling —went on, I saw that they were as ghost-ridden in some ways as I, certainly haunted enough to be anxious in their deceptive sexual "freedom." The conflicts, the contrasts between their lives in the heat of the Dominican tropics and Norte-americano cool, the experimentation of their relationships and the rigid values of their parents, were troubling.

I remember Carolyn vividly: she was an accomplished and capable woman in her mid-twenties who had put together a major child-care program in remote mountain communities while living for two years in a palm-thatched hut without running water. As her tour of duty came to an end and she faced returning home, her increasing uneasiness was apparent to all. Her main concern? She was no longer a virgin, and she was afraid that her mother, with the mystical power with which children endow their parents, would somehow sense her "downfall." She knew in no uncertain terms that she was expected to remain a virgin until a wedding ring was securely in place on her finger, and the feeling that she'd disappointed and contravened her mother's expectations was so strong that she vowed she would move to another city after a short stay at home. I had long thought of Carolyn as a sexual revolutionary, one who would be able to cross the divide and communicate with her parents about her choice, but I realized that, faced with her mother's censoriousness, she did what I, sexual conservative, would have done in the same position. She ran.

Nancy Friday writes about the "chain of gender" that keeps us imprisoned in old notions of who we are sexually. "There is a clue here to the conservative backlash so often found in children of women who proclaim themselves sexually liberated. The daughter does not so much take in the mother's brisk new chatter about freedom as she is conforming to the deep, often unconscious feelings about sex mother learned as a little girl herself. It takes more than a generation to change the lessons we learn through our mothers." [11] This is borne out by studies of women who had premarital sex: they don't express remorse and they would repeat the experience given the choice. But they expect their daughters to conform to a more conservative ethic.

The results of a *Redbook* survey of 100,000 mothers, most of whom had premarital intercourse, demonstrate this conflict: 12 percent said they objected to premarital sex for their sons; 24 percent objected to that prospect for their daughters.[12] Perhaps because these women defied sexual prohibitions and the rules of their own parents, they may carry residual guilt, which breaks out in disapproval of more liberal stances: "Do what I say, not what I do." To prove that she is not a Bad Girl, a woman laden with this guilt makes her daughter a *very* Good Girl. She wants to believe her daughter will be stronger than she was to make up for her transgression of her parents' trust in her.

Her own experience notwithstanding, the mother who herself had been sexually adventurous seems to respond to the voices in her past (that she ignored *then*) warning her to keep a tight rein on her sexual feelings, or suffer the consequences due a Bad Girl. She remembers the risks of premarital sex: if her daughter errs in her judgment about a man's intentions, it can lead to her undoing in the marriage—i.e., security—market. Never mind that this dire future was not the mother's; she was "lucky," but she wants to ensure that her daughter does not have to depend on luck.

One of the questions I asked people concerned their daughters' sexuality: at what age and under what circumstances would it be all right for one's child to have sexual intercourse? All of the women (and a high proportion of the men) indicated that emotional involvement was the watershed: "In a longtime, continuing relationship of love and caring"; "When she's had prior positive and successful relationships"; "I would hope that the relationship isn't casual"; "There should be feelings of love and commitment with mutual sharing"; "*Only* if she knew there would be a future [marriage] with the male." The fear seems to be that daughters won't recognize the importance of following the sequence: emotional involvement as a desired precedent to sexual experience. It's a value that is at once a projection of the mother's own needs and an enforcement of the cultural norm. Unfortunately, too often the message is transmitted as "Sex is bad; *you* are bad if you indulge in sex with an improper partner." Our culture has embedded such deep images about proper sexual behavior that it is unlikely that mothers will be free enough for generations to applaud their daughters' sexual experiences.

I find myself as ambivalent as the next mother. Despite my protestations of liberation, I have difficulty accepting that my daughter could develop a mature and self-protecting sexual ethic of her own. *I* want to protect her, I want her to find a man who treats her honorably. I want to save her the pain of making the mistakes that I made. It breaks my heart to possess all this hard-won knowledge that she seems unable to use. I have to stand back and bite my tongue to keep myself from warning her, "Be careful. Don't . . ."

SEX AND THE SINGLE (WIDOWED, DIVORCED) MOTHER

My mother is 46, and she was recently divorced. I'm afraid that she won't be able to deal with the sexual revolution. She has no idea what guys are like today. Mom says she intends to date and have all the fun she hasn't had in years. I just hope she remembers she is a grandmother and needs to set a good example for her granddaughter.

Jeannette, 28

The strength of social control is in its self-perpetuation: Jeanette is as effective a control agent toward her mother as her mother is to her. Most daughters, even those with the very best of liberal intentions, find themselves assuming a protective role when their mothers become newly single.

A recent Phil Donahue show examined the trend of senior citizens setting up relationships outside of marriage, of living together. The intensity with which some of the daughters (all middle-aged) expressed their dismay and disapproval at these arrangements was surprising. One said: "*My* mother would never do *that*." Donahue pressed her: Do what? "My mother is a good woman," she replied, as if that covered everything. Even grandmothers on the recycled singles circuit are subject to the norms of "good" behavior.

THE ENFORCERS

Guilt is our common female denominator, the internal police that keep us in line, one way our society enforces sexual standards. We punish *ourselves* with guilt when we break society's rules, hoping against hope to evade public retribution. Guilt is the mechanism that makes internal policing effective. There are so many things we aren't supposed to do about sex that we find ourselves constantly in conflict. A girl learns by "continued pressure, transmitted at first by peers and parents and later by the girl herself, to act like and become a 'nice girl.' "[13]

Unfortunately, the status of "nice" or "good" is one that must be constantly achieved: every action a woman takes is susceptible to judgment. "One's identity as 'lady' or 'nice girl' is never finally confirmed. Rather, it is continually in jeopardy, and one is under pressure to demonstrate one's niceness anew by one's behavior in each instance of social interaction. . . . There is no front stage/back stage dichotomy with normative control. Women are 'on' whenever and wherever they are, whether in the company of men, strangers, or other women. More important, however, is the expectation that a woman will be nice or good when she is by herself."[14] It's quite a role, being "good." And so demanding that it effectively removes a woman from arenas where good or nice is of no value: those competitive, aggressive male spheres of business, politics, finance.

The flip side of continually trying to be good is that any failure, any lapse from approved behavior, can *permanently* relegate a woman to the status of Bad: Hester Prynne's scarlet A is no less traumatic than a woman's *self*-perception as unworthy. And even a lapse that is unknown in a wider context will affect a woman's sense of self. *To be free from this guilt is the crux of a woman's struggle to find her true sexuality.*

Young girls learn to be moral enforcers: they have a great responsibility because if sex takes place, it's a girl's fault. Boys can't be responsible; it's their masculine nature to want sex; they are sexually impulsive and can't curb their appetite. So it's up to the female to keep the ravening male at bay. And if you think this attitude went out with waist cinchers and stiletto heels, let me remind you that all of these antediluvian tortures are enjoying a revival.

Therapist Natalie Mackler discussed the torments women put themselves through when they feel they've failed their own (socially implanted) expectations: "Women feel shame when they break their own rules. It's an internal measure that relates to self-image. Guilt is another way of measuring your own failings: it often appears when you 'get caught' or are afraid that what you did and feel ashamed of will be exposed."

Fear of exposure keeps us in line; we're afraid someone might find out, that what we do in the privacy of our bedrooms somehow shows. As a young girl I thought that losing your virginity made you as bowlegged as a cowboy. And Natalie Mackler remembers a similar superstition: "We were standing in line waiting to go to the movies, a couple of my girlfriends and I, and ahead of us was a classmate we knew had had sex. There was a large pimple on her nose and we all agreed, 'See, you can tell she's not a virgin.' We never get over the feeling that our secrets about sex will be discovered and we'll be labeled, discounted."

"I slept with the man I later married," an attorney in her thirties wrote, "but I was eaten up with guilt until the ring was on my finger and I was running down the front steps of the church under a shower of rice." And a woman I struck up a conversation with in an airport had a unique twist on self-policing. "I first had sex at sixteen," she said. "I looked at the whole virginity routine as a bore and a burden. I manage to enjoy sex and keep most of the old 'dont's' way in the back of my head. But every now and then I notice a twinge of something I've finally begun to identify as guilt. I'm not sure where it all comes from, but from time to time, in a crazy way, I feel a little guilty about *not* feeling guilty about having sex." She felt she would be a better person—a Good Girl—if she suffered at least a little because she had been sexual.

Nancy Friday discovered that the notion of being good is so all-encompassing that we even police our fantasy lives. "In over seven years of research on women's sexual fantasies, the most prevalent themes I found were rape, domination and force. Good Girls to the end, we made the other person *do it* to us. I want to say this emphatically: not a single woman I ever talked to said she wanted to be raped in actuality. What is wanted is something only in the imagination, *release from the responsibility of sex."* [15]

THE SIN SYNDROME

> It was a sin for you to want to feel up Ellen.
> It was a sin for you to plan to feel up Ellen.
> It was a sin for you to figure out a place to
>   feel up Ellen.
> It was a sin to take Ellen to the place to
>   feel her up.
> It was a sin to try to feel her up, and it
>   was a sin to feel her up.
> It was six sins in one feel, man.
>
> *George Carlin* [16]

In my Catholic girlhood, sin was easily discernible and quantifiable, and it had a great deal to do with sex. For our First Holy Communion we dressed like little brides, all in white; confirmation wed us to Jesus, a ceremony we secretly sealed with cigar-band wedding rings. The rigidity and absoluteness of Catholic dogma drove me wild, and I clashed regularly and fiercely with Father O'Keefe in catechism class, confounding him (I thought) with my twelve-year-old's sophistries. "Father O'Keefe, if riding a boy's bicycle is a temptation to sin, what if it's the only way to get to mass on Sunday?'' Only boy's bikes were forbidden, and I didn't figure out the reason until I was long past bike-riding age. That crossbar was considered a devil in disguise, a tantalizing attraction for the all-too-susceptible genitalia of budding female sexuality.

The Legion of Decency kept a sharp eye on our morals, and once a week we recited the pledge. I was infatuated with being another St. Bernadette (I'd seen the movie *Song of Bernadette*), so I gave it my pious all: "I pledge to see good, wholesome movies. I will not see movies that endanger my immortal salvation. . . ." Those movies were not objectionable, they were *forbidden*. Otto Preminger's *The Moon Is Blue*, for instance, a slender comedy about a virgin and her determined suitors, was banned for its slightly risqué portrayal of sex and profanity: the words "damn" and "hell," and "virgin" uttered out loud without connecting it to Mary. To see *any* Ingrid Bergman movie (that fallen woman) was to jeopardize one's very soul, but, always jesuitical, I *read* everything I could about her, devouring the details of her illicit love affair. I didn't venture into a movie theater even to see *Casablanca* until long after I was a safely married woman and consequently, in the eyes of the church, no longer subject to Bergman's corrupting influence.[17]

Sex was totally forbidden except in marriage for procreation. Simple, straightforward interdictions. But, with the cheerful equivocation of the young, I softened the prohibitions. Necking and petting were Little Sins and only slightly dangerous— a few hundred years in purgatory at worst. I could probably offer up enough Hail Marys to pray my way out. Intercourse was a Big Sin: decades of Decades (*ten* Hail Marys), fasting, and haircloth shirts would not be sufficient penitence to keep me out of hell for committing a mortal sin of that magnitude. If peer-group pressure and parental values were not enough to convince me to conform, Mother Church's dicta were added to the other codes that bound me squarely in the ranks of the good.

The Catholic Church certainly doesn't have a corner on sex

as a sin. A friend who grew up in a fundamentalist family described her church's lessons. "The evils of sex was the number one topic for the pastor's fiery sermonizing. He would glare around the room and accuse the congregation, 'Sinners, you are all sinners. You lust; I know you have sinned over lust.' " And Sunday after Sunday from the electronic pulpits of the Christian broadcasting networks, preacher after preacher condemns the grave danger of the Satanic temptation of premarital sex. Those of us raised with religious strictures against sex may find shaking those early teachings harder than any other changes we make in our lives. Even if a woman believes her attitudes and actions are right and proper, an entire body of judges, the congregation and religious officials of her church, stand together every sabbath to contradict her.

Fear of punishment for transgressing by being sexual—i.e., female—has been a cornerstone or normative control since Eve's lust was blamed for bringing down the wrath of God on all mankind. Religion authorizes this attitude through a higher power than just social custom: the word of God. But, lest we forget, it is God's word as interpreted by society's rulemakers —men—with vested interests (in economy and posterity) in constraining women to remain Good Girls.

So we are taught that we have lousy judgment. We learn to obey the rules and not to question the wisdom of the stern rulemakers. We are taught at an early age not to trust our own impulses, to deny our sensuality, to submit our actions to approval from others before they can become valid. No wonder our sexual decision-making is faulty, our critical faculties impaired. If we admit to desiring what *feels* good, pleasurable, and natural, we are branded as Bad Girls. To *be* good, we must deny or repress what we want.

The result, Elizabeth Janeway writes, is that "the societal restraints imposed on women by the stereotypes of our culture have cost us an enormous amount of psychic energy. How much talent and capacity must have been wasted in holding our impulses down, in molding our behavior to match the ideal our consciences held up as appropriate to the good woman! How often, and how intensely, we have quarreled with ourselves when we begin to feel the urge to act in some insidious unwomanly way, just because it would be pleasing to us instead of being good for others."[18]

BAD GIRLS FINISH FIRST

Here is a quick look at a Bad Girl as described by an anonymous forty-year-old: "The bad girl cares more about herself than anyone else. She is selfishly indulgent, she says goodbye to many men, she is likely to be divorced three times. She does exactly as she pleases. She likes sex and expresses her desires through actions and words. She is intelligent and usually a professional woman. She is not self-sacrificing." This from a self-professed Good Girl. It's a picture of a pretty strong woman, and except for those three divorces, I'd rather be Bad!

5

LEARNING THE RULES

THE NOT-SO-FABULOUS FIFTIES

"Please don't, you're going too far," Good Girl after Good Girl murmured to insistent boyfriends in my youth. I was a teenager in the 1950s, and the message I received about being female was explicit: Don't have intercourse before marriage or you'll lose your reputation. The warning had a direct bearing on my life, as I spent night after night entangled with my high school boyfriend, Terry, in the back seat of his red convertible, locked in what seemed like an eternal battle of the erogenous combat zones: above the waist, below the waist, under the blouse, etc. I wanted Terry, but I wanted my reputation too, so each date became a fight to the finish. When Terry finally graduated, my virginity was intact, but my reputation, alas, was not. It was subtle, but I recognized the change: solicitous inquiries like, "Are you two engaged?" and "Are you 'okay' [not pregnant]?"

To this day, I have no idea if Terry boasted of our "going all the way" or people simply assumed, because we were parked in that lonely little convertible so much, that one thing had led to another. And damn it, I still care. At my twenty-fifth high school reunion it was all I could do not to march up to the stage, grab the microphone, and announce, "I did not—repeat, did *not*—sleep with Terry." I graduated from high school a virgin, I married as a virgin, and some real throwback in my psyche still wants full credit for obeying the rules even though I don't believe in them at all anymore.

What kept me and the majority of my classmates in line was fear; I wasn't good by choice. It wasn't easy hanging on to my virtue, between the importuning from the likes of Terry and my body's own demands. But to succeed in 1950 at getting a man—and in 1950, our futures *were* our men—we had to preserve ourselves for Mr. Right. Each of us had a hidden agenda. A girl wanted evidence that she could "get" a guy, so she mastered the art of leading him to a frenzy, then abruptly withdrawing, demanding to go home. The more he wanted her, the more dates she got. And dates were our gold medals, our proof that we were desirable, popular, and feminine. So we might engage in semi-sex, bending the rules, but we remained "technical" virgins. Once the line was crossed and the hymen punctured, marriage had better be in the future, the immediate future.

The girl who broke this convention was labeled, objectified; her value as a person was attacked. Cheap. Trash. Terms applied to worthless commodities. Whore. Slut. The very violence of the words hurled at women who didn't profess remorse at having sex without the legal sanction of marriage shows how threatening the power of uncontained female sexuality can be. The harsh judgment behind those overwrought epithets is a clue to the sizable investment our culture has made in keeping women Good Girls.

There *were* breaks in the ranks: between 1948 and 1960, the number of women who had premarital sex increased steadily. But it wasn't casual; more than half of these women reported that they had only one sexual partner, their fiancé. If a woman wasn't engaged, or engaged to be engaged, she had sex away from home and parental disapproval. Sex, said the women in Kinsey's 1953 study, only takes place in serious relationships.[1]

SEX IN THE SIXTIES

Penny was seventeen in 1965; her sexual maturity and the sexual revolution coincided, but she recalls that the earliest messages she received about how to behave were as stringent as the ones fed me over a decade before. "There was definitely a division based on chastity, on innocence. Good Girls wore Kotex, for instance, and bad ones wore Tampax because you had to touch yourself 'down there' to insert them. And we assumed that you couldn't be a virgin and wear a tampon.

"The *appearance* of righteousness was extremely important. Never mind that dates inevitably ended on golf courses, by the lake, in the mountains—we were too poor and too scared to go to motels—where we stroked our boyfriends to climax or offered blow jobs to ease their self-proclaimed agony of 'blue balls.' By night, we satisfied their biological needs without compromising our reputations. By day, we were perfect little virgins. We saw the way boys treated 'fast' girls, and I for one learned never to expose myself to that humiliation and cruelty."

In the late sixties, women began to rebel against the old rules and the strictures against premarital sex weakened. Women were likely to have sex in affectionate relationships, but usually it was serial monogamy. A woman who wasn't having sex before marriage wasn't saving herself for Mr. Right anymore, she simply didn't have a man in her life. Chastity became a near artifact, and most of us would agree with historian John Fluegel on the subject: "The most charitable thing we can say about chastity is that it is useless; and that, if we look at the matter closely, those who lead chaste lives appear to be the victims of an illusion. Chastity merits neither admiration, praise nor criticism. There are people who have a large appetite, others who have a moderate one, still others who have no appetite at all; it is a personal affair. To turn it into a question of right and wrong is surely a most lamentable outcome of false reasoning."[2]

Interestingly, in the late 1940s and 1950s, 20 percent of college males reported sexual experience with prostitutes. By 1960, that figure had dropped to 4 percent.[3] Men were having sex with friends, with classmates, women they knew—with Good Girls. Men and women began to live together in relationships outside of marriage in such vast numbers that the U.S. Census Bureau had to coin the impossibly jargonistic term POSSLQ (Persons of Opposite Sex Sharing Living Quarters) to report on households. Clearly, the world was becoming more permissive.

THE SEXY SEVENTIES

The seventies spoke a new language. Me, Self, Disco, Woody Allen, "I'm OK, You're OK," Sex. Mostly sex. These were, as one reviewer put it, "the years in which you could get away with it. . . . You want to roller-skate to work, have an abortion, come out of the closet . . . see *Deep Throat* four times? Go ahead."[4] The sexual revolution was really on a roll. The stirrings of changes in our sexual behavior, which began in the sixties on the fringes of society, were now mainstream. Studies in the mid-1950s reported that only 33 percent of all twenty-five-year-old women had sex before marriage. Now twenty years later, a most respectable magazine, *Redbook*, told us that nine out of ten of its women readers reported having sex before marriage. Another survey found that between 1971 and 1976 there had been a 30 percent increase in the number of teenaged girls between fifteen and nineteen years old who were sexually active. Even parents became more tolerant about sex before marriage. In a 1979 poll, 63 percent of parents said it was all right. Contrast this to 1967, when the same pollsters were told by 85 percent of the parents of college-age students that premarital sex was morally wrong.[5]

The unraveling of the old cloth that had bound up female sexuality may have begun when feminists marched down Fifth Avenue on a cold January day in 1976 to kick off the decade of women. But no matter trying to pinpoint it, optimism was the theme of the day. "The discovery, or we should say validation, of a joyous, assertive, and distinctly female sexuality seemed to promise that feminism would liberate women sexually as well as politically and socially."[6]

Not only was the lid off female sexuality, women were even *encouraged* to be sexy. An avalanche of books and magazine articles gave explicit instructions for achieving sexual fulfillment: venturing into new positions, saying yes to oral sex, always going for orgasm (preferably multiple), exploring one's own body ("solo sex" or "self-pleasuring," depending on the expert giving the advice). The end of sexual dysfunction was reported to be imminent. You could hardly avoid the talk of women's untapped sexual prowess, even if you tried.

But why, we can ask, were so many women walking around in skin-tight jeans with someone else's name embroidered on their buttocks? And why were so many willing to totter about on three-inch heels with a signature over their toes declaring them to be a candied confection? Best selling books such as *The Total Woman, Fascinating Womanhood,* and *Be a Woman,*[7] antidotes to the new feminism, preached the doctrine of domesticity and sex appeal as the way to hold on to a man— woman as combination of the Happy Homemaker and a Playboy Bunny. It was confusion passed off in most circles as paradox. Others saw the shifts and reshifts as part of a process. Gloria Steinem wrote, "Of course, massive change proceeds more as a spiral than a straight line. We repeat similar patterns over and over again, each time in a slightly different circumstance, so experiences that appear to be circular and discouraging in the short run may turn out to be moving in a clear direction in the long run."[8]

PLUS ÇA CHANGE... THE EXCRUCIATING EIGHTIES

My expectation was that I would find a much more relaxed standard of behavior among college women and high school girls today, and I was sorely disappointed. Nineteen-year-old Julie wrote about her perception of the rules today: "If a man doesn't have sex, he is labeled queer or abnormal. But if a girl *does*, she has to be careful that she doesn't get labeled the town whore. We're freer to say yes, but I was brought up to say no. I feel guilty about sleeping with a man I'm not married to."

Ann, who is sixteen, agrees that there are different rules for boys and girls. "In my high school lots of kids have sex, and everyone knows it. It's okay as long as a girl and a guy are going out together. But if a girl has sex with too many guys, she'll get a reputation for being sleazy. It's a bummer, and the guys pretend they don't care, but if you don't watch out, they start saying you're sleazy."

An anonymous psychology student in North Carolina struck the most regressive note; her comment reminded me painfully of the standards of my own day. "The double standard is far from being obsolete. It really makes me angry to think that in a sense it encourages male promiscuity, which can lead to difficulties in starting a relationship. It also says that females can't enjoy sex or else they are 'loose,' 'easy,' etc. Even in an unmarried love relationship, the man 'has it good,' but no one better find out that the girl is sleeping with her boyfriend."

It's bad enough to have to worry about being branded "too easy," "sleazy." Now, another bauble has been added to our worry beads: We must consider our partner's sexual history and take stock of our own. A bleak fact of life today is the threat of AIDS and the appearance of other STDs (chlamydia, for example) that weren't around in our coming-of-age days.

THE GREAT DIVIDE

Promiscuous: Anyone who's having more sex than you are.
                                                "San Antonio," 34

I had a laugh at this cynical definition from a woman at a lecture in Texas, but she had a point. What's good (and who's good) shifts with the prevailing moral wind. But some constraints remain constant: uncontrolled female sexuality leads to trouble in our society, and there is some line over which a woman steps that changes her from good to bad.

Virginity was traditionally the line. Besides the obvious plus of indisputable paternity, the fallacy that the more pure a woman before her marriage, the more faithful afterward, has lingered for a long time. According to traditional standards, premarital intercourse is wrong. Simple and to the point. For centuries, moralists and theologians have argued that sex and marriage *must* go together because offspring need the security that a stable, contractual relationship provides: a mother, a father, a legitimate family life and parental devotion. Fornication was immoral in the most pragmatic sense because of potential deleterious effects if a child was conceived. With the invention of reliable contraception, one might assume that the cultural value of virginity and the arguments against premarital sex would have disappeared.[9]

But a study of 4,000 men between the ages of eighteen and sixty-five proved otherwise. Thirty-two percent of the men polled preferred that their wives have no sexual experience with other men. While older men were more likely to opt for virgins (51 percent of the men over fifty-five) than men in their thirties (27 percent),[10] and the desire for a chaste partner was expressed as a wish rather than an expectation, that wish still exists contrary to all the words, words, words about the sexual revolution.

Maybe this antique wish is rooted in a man's sense of himself. Theo Lang, an authority on human sexuality, explains: "Like the cellophane wrapping on a candy bar or the seal on a letter it [virginity] shows that he has received goods 'untouched by hand,' or knowledge unknown to others. Man's virgin bride becomes an individual possession and consequently enhances his status as a select and unique individual."[11] A co-worker in the field had another theory. "Maybe," she said, "there's a practical explanation for the old wistfulness for an 'untouched' woman. A virgin can't compare sexual partners; she doesn't know the difference between a great lover and an inadequate one."

Men know realistically that the women they are intimate with will have had prior experience. But there is still a limit to the *amount* of experience that's acceptable, still no single standard for both sexes. That won't apply until there are *no* social or psychological controls applied differently to men and women. Interviewee Jossie knows: "I really don't feel we've hit the stage where there is simply no difference in erotic possibilities for men and women. Women still have to be much more careful than men, much more discreet and selective. It's still more okay for a man to be sexual than a woman."

> In general, I'm not impressed with the stereotypical promiscuous woman. She (the stereotype; I'm sure there are exceptions) seems to me to be shallow. And maybe I'm a hopeless romantic, but I want a relationship to be special. I don't just want to be one of the crowd.
>
> *Larry, 37*

Larry is not alone in his attitude. A Minnesota doctor's criteria are equally one-sided and old-fashioned. "You can't use numerical equations to determine how many lovers you feel the woman you are serious about [read "Good Girl"] should have had. I just have the feeling that if a woman is too casual about sex, she'll be too casual about having sex with me." I've heard the terminology "relatively unused" (sounds like a car!) applied to what men want. "Single women intuitively understand this principle of putting out their favors in limited editions and develop mythological sexual histories, elevating pleasant friendships to deep loves and expurgating minor characters; some women permit themselves to add an additional meaningful relationship to the saga with every few birthdays." [12]

Walt, a forty-five-year-old computer programmer, talks about his wistful desire for an old-fashioned "nice" girl coupled with a desire for a sexy bedmate. "I know it's a contradiction, thinking it would be nice to marry a woman who is a virgin, yet I want a woman who knows how to enjoy a good time in bed. This doesn't mean I want a woman who has been promiscuous. I'm flattered when a woman comes on to me, but I wonder if she's not just a little too forward." He waited until I had written down what he said, and added, "I mean that a woman shouldn't be shy about sex, but not reckless about it. If she does sleep around, she has to use discretion."

Men prefer not to hear the whole truth. They'd rather be told that there weren't "that many" other loves, and never "anyone like you." Remember the scene in *Carnal Knowledge* when Ann-Margret tells Art Garfunkel her past? "You wanted to know," she says, and he wails, "But I didn't know there would be so many."

"A woman's past must be kept to a minimum," says Linda Blocki, editor-in-chief of *Singles Scene Magazine*. "During her mid-twenties, a woman often sits down and makes a list of all the men she has had sex with. When she can't remember a man's name but can remember his face, it begins to strike fear into her heart. She hides the list. She goes back to it and reprimands herself. . . . And then another man comes along, and mentally she adds him to her list. Yet I've never met a man who makes a list for the reason of keeping himself under control."

A reporter in her early thirties felt that "women who have had a number of sexual experiences have to downplay them. We know we don't have to be virgins anymore to 'hook' a guy, but you'd be a fool to flaunt your experience. Men want sexy women, but they don't want women who've been sexy with great legions of men."

"We have been taught to expect that men have a lot of experience. It is because men who have a lot of experience are better lovers and we feel we can benefit? Why can't men use the same logic? Can't they see that a woman with experience will be a better lover?" rejoined another member of an audience I was talking to in New Orleans. We were working toward a definition of "too much," a codification of the new rules, a mapping of the contemporary boundary line between

Good and Bad. A young woman stood up and asked, "Why do women have to make the adjustment? This makes me so mad; it's just one more area where women are supposed to play dumb." Unfortunately, our society still conditions men to think there is something wrong with an obviously sexually experienced woman.

One way a man may surmount his conflict between his need for the woman he loves to be sexually inexperienced and the reality that she no longer is, is by resorting to the myth of the woman unfulfilled. According to the myth, only an inspired lover—himself—can fully arouse the woman. She may have been sexually active, but she certainly couldn't have enjoyed it. His prowess in the role of her lover will finally enable her to achieve satisfaction. Once again, a male granting permission to a woman to be fully sexual.

THE NEW NOES

All of this leaves women confused. What is it that men want? How many *is* too many? What are the rules? Women who have had two or three lovers worry that they are promiscuous, while others who have had dozens worry that they aren't adventurous enough. Trying to get a handle on what's good or bad today, I began asking in workshop sessions and on questionnaires for descriptions of messages, implied or stated, that shape feminine behavior. As I collated the responses, one thing became clear: premarital intercourse appeared as a "don't" on all of the lists. The restrictions varied with the age of the woman, but there was always some negative attached. Older women leaned toward condemning all sex outside of marriage. Younger women, while more flexible, were still conditional. Their answers appeared liberal at first, but stringent qualifiers were attached: "*If* you are going steady with the guy," "*if* you love him," etc. A strong echo of Kinsey's (1950s) findings: "We only have sex in serious relationships." Serial monogamy rather than premarital chastity emerged as the new standard. And within this liberal ethic there are still acceptable and unacceptable ways for a woman to behave sexually.

Despite constant disclaimers—there are no rules, sex is an individual experience, women are as free as men to express their sexuality—the following are the most prevalent restrictions I encountered:

A woman should *not*
   have too many men;
   be too eager or acrobatic;
   be too passive;
   give sexual instructions until she knows her partner; or
   be too prepared (i.e., take a diaphragm on a date).

A woman *should*
   be responsive to her partner;
   let him turn her on;
   be discreet about past sexual experiences; and
   be discreet about birth control.

What a stew of conflicting feelings; it's amazing that a woman doesn't just succumb to paralysis trying to accommodate them. In an era that purports to be sexually free, everyone seemed to have a few rules to curtail that freedom.

But our confusion about how to be sexy but not *too* sexy is understandable because we are living in a time of transition and the rules tend to change in the middle of the game. Natalie Mackler describes our new standard. "The message has changed over the years. It used to be 'Be good.' Now we're told 'Be good, but if you can't be good, be careful.' But who hears 'Be careful' as giving permission? And 'Be good' is still the first rule."

6

THE REVOLUTIONARY FAÇADE

ON THE ROAD TO FREEDOM

The sexual revolution was a product of the Pill and the women's movement. Virtually foolproof contraception, backed up by legalized abortion, meant that for the first time in history we could control our fertility without the knowledge and/or cooperation of men. Our bodies could truly belong to us. It was earth-shaking; in the early 1970s when I gave talks on birth control methods around the country, older women in the audience applauded when I brought out the Pill. They'd lived with the uncertainties of ineffective contraceptive methods; they *knew* what a tremendous freedom that tiny pink or yellow or blue tablet offered.

Shere Hite helped us enjoy this newfound freedom when she dispelled the myth of the "vaginal" orgasm and announced that the clitoris was the chief site of a woman's erotic sensation. And furthermore, Masters and Johnson acknowledged that women's sexual potential was at least equal to men's. What a breakthrough in one decade: we achieved the technology, the know-how, and the *permission* to be sexually active and fulfilled human beings.

The women's liberation movement gave us the backbone to

demand sexual pleasure; it taught us it was our *right* to partic-
ipate in and enjoy sex on an equal basis with men. Just as it
was our right to hold the same job as a man and receive equal
pay for equal work.

Social structures began to change. It used to be easy to get
married and difficult to get divorced. Now divorce is a way of
life (nearly one out of every two marriages in the United States
ends in divorce)[1] and marriage is considered a difficult step to
take. Women work, childbearing is delayed, single men and
women change apartments and partners without even a
glance from the neighbors.

We have a lot more choices than we used to: in education,
careers, personal relationships. The pressure is on to be self-
sufficient. There's no longer the image of the lonely spinster
sharing a one-room studio with her cat or parakeet, trudging
off to an unrewarding job day in and day out. "Spinster" just
sounds outdated: "single," on the other hand, rings with excitement. It sounds unfettered, free, dynamic.

BEHIND THE FAÇADE

Now it is more or less recognized that women have sexual needs
and should be free to express these needs without guilt and fear.
The problem I find, though, is that no one seems to understand
that I have feelings and emotions that biologically or psychologically are still tied up with the sex act and have *not* undergone a
revolution. Maybe it's because I'm the one who will physically
bear the baby. Who knows? All I know is that I feel frustrated
trying to deny my vulnerable feelings.

Marya, 24

Although living in an era of sexual freedom, we don't feel—
and so are not—free. Sexual liberation fills us with ambivalence. We remain caught between the old ideas of sex (Good
Girls don't) and the new ones (fulfilled women do). Our vision

of our sexual selves is blurred: "I know I'm supposed to be free to sleep with any man I want, but I feel stigmatized if I give in too easily. I have never approached a man; I'm too old-fashioned," wrote a college senior on a questionnaire. Alice, twenty-two, characterized her version of the sexual revolution. " 'Hi! My name is Alice. Wanna screw?' " she said. "We're so damn cool. I've had a lot of sex, I wanted to see what it was all about, and most of it was lousy."

James McCary notes that "a true sexual revolution involves a dramatic change in the attitudes and ethics governing sexual behavior as well as in the behavior itself. Conclusive evidence of such a change does not yet exist, but there are signs that the trend is in that direction. Overall, the most significant change has been in sexual attitudes, and the changes are most pronounced among young women. *Their liberal attitudes about sex are rapidly approaching those of young men's.*"[2]

Alice, Marya, and an anonymous college student: three of McCary's "young women of liberal attitudes"? Only if liberal is synonymous with disillusioned.

The pain and confusion are greater for older women. Jayne, a forty-four-year-old school nurse, wrote about trying to come to grips with the changing world. "In my age range, expectations of women and men about love and sex are different. But *I* think men have gained more from the sexual revolution than women have: now they can have 'live-ins' to do the chores. I think men are the takers and women are the givers. I'm glad that a young woman today doesn't have the terrible guilt I used to; I hope the sexual revolution has at least done that. I could never be casual about sex; I'm a role model for three teenage girls. I think others live by a more casual sexual code than I could agree with."

Part of the reason for the disorientation we're suffering from is that changes in attitude and behavior are not necessarily congruent. Behavior changes, when they occur, usually lag behind attitudinal changes by ten years.

Author Janet Harris sees another reason for the lag. "Values, goals, life-styles for women in American society change just often enough to prevent each new generation of women from identifying with any previous ones."[3] It's a matter of role models: in these shifting times we can't depend on what our mothers did to be right for us now. And there is a sad lack of female role models in the public eye. So every day women face new ambiguities, complexities, and difficulties, judging new choices against old familiar routines, and we feel we're facing all these decisions alone. We wish that somewhere there existed an ultimate set of rules we should adhere to, a sort of Emily Post of "proper" sexual etiquette.

What is "proper" sexual behavior is written in sand, not carved in granite. All of our ideas about nudity, virginity, fidelity, love, marriage, men and women are meaningful only within our particular cultural context. Behavior that is labeled "moral" or "immoral" differs from one era to another. We now appear to be sparring partners in a whole new arena of sexual conduct and expectations, but the rules have yet to be written: "I feel like I'm caught in the sexual revolution. When I was in college (1960s) and in my twenties, everyone felt free to have all the sex she wanted. Now it seems there's a return to more caution and prudence. Or maybe it's a change inside me." This from a New York lawyer, who, like all of us, is feeling her way in the dark.

Part of our disappointment stems from our thought that the advent of women's liberation would help free us from the oppression of sexual stereotypes, from gamesmanship, from the rules of being Good Girls. And while it did teach us our worth, it was *not* about the sexual revolution per se. "From an historical perspective, there are some good reasons for our present confusion. Nowhere is it written that women's liberation and sexual liberation go hand in hand. In fact, over the decades, the relationship between the two has been on again, off again, with more time spent in hostile separation than conjugal peace."[4]

The women's movement taught us that we are *more* than

our sexuality, that biology is not destiny and gender is incidental in fulfilling one's potential as a human. And if it is true that it gave us the right to enjoy sex, it also gave us the right to refuse it: "I used to have sex because I had to prove I was liberated," was the way a respondent in her mid-thirties put it. "A man could make you feel frigid or inadequate if you didn't just want to sleep with him. But I'm getting assertive. I don't feel that I have to have sex unless I want to. And when I say no, I mean it." More and more women are turning to another part of the anatomy—the brain—to achieve the commodities women used to be granted under the old trade-off of sex for a wedding ring.

THE BIG SELL?

If women had won the sexual revolution, there would be no such thing as casual sex.

Kathy, 33

Psychiatrists, sex therapists, books, television, movies, and advertising flash the high sign to enjoy sex. Best-sellers proclaim *How to Make Love to a Man* and *Nice Girls Do.* Ads hint at what to wear "when you leave home on Sunday and won't be back 'til Monday." Even sherry commercials, once the province of maiden aunts, now show a sexy woman in a low-cut dress with a wicked twinkle in her eye and a proposition on her lips. "Come over for a drink," she purrs. But all of this can feel like a big sell, devoted to keeping us happy as we leap from bed to bed and men wallow in heretofore unbelievable sexual possibilities.

Women haven't really been freed by all this so-called sexual revolution. Sure, we're freer to say yes than we used to be, but we are still raised not to have premarital sex, or to feel guilty

when we do. Men are not taught that they shouldn't have sex.
They don't experience a guilt trip all the time about sex.

Susan, 20

Susan's complaint sounds like a distillation of hundreds of
others from women of all ages. Shere Hite has noted that "the
change in women's role was double-edged."[5] Anthropologists
and sociologists who study trends and patterns of human interaction have identified measurable behavioral changes that
define the sexual revolution in its broadest cultural sense, and
the changes tilt the sexual balance of power in favor of the
masculine world. Women now have sex before marriage with
more than one man, and cohabitation no longer leads to the
expectation of marriage. What this means is that men have
been freed to sleep with Good Girls without the time-honored
obligation of exchanging security and access to their power
and wealth. The sexual revolution freed men to have sexual
intercourse with Good Girls without any strings attached. *It
did not—or has not yet—provided Good Girls with the upbringing,
rewards, or even necessarily the desire, to reciprocate.*

The ideology of the sexual revolution promotes the concept of
spontaneous sex, sex without strings, any time, with any partner, for physical pleasure. A desire to connect feelings with sex
is considered old-fashioned, socially backward, even neurotic.
Have we women *really* experienced a sexual revolution? Or are
men and women using free sex to obscure their need for more
meaningful relationships and to avoid examining the shallow-
ness of their lives?

Helen, 39

We want sexual choices, but we don't want sex without
intimacy. *The Hite Report* found that few women want uncom-
mitted sex very often, although some believed that they ought
to want it and would be happier if they did.[6] Sexual freedom
to a woman means the right to conduct her sexual life as she

sees fit rather than at the dictates of society or a man. But to men it seems to mean licentiousness, a flight from intimacy. This man's confusion is typical: "Why are women, given the sexual freedom we have now, still so hung up on love and—capital 'R'—relationships? The women I know don't enjoy their freedom at all; they all want to go back to the old love and marriage days."

Overwhelmingly, women still want sex to have some meaning, to be connected to a relationship that includes love and a future. Louise, nineteen, described her disappointment at a recent failure to connect with a man any way other than sexually: "I expected something more; intimacy, sharing, an opening of selves." And Laurie, an administrator in a health care program, described how she feels about sex and commitment: "It's conceivable that I could go to bed with a guy for pure pleasure, but I'm looking for that total package. I'm looking for intelligence and humor as well as chemistry. Sex is important but you can't base everything on it."

We don't feel that the so-called revolution has added substantially to our lives because our underlying desire is to be loved for ourselves, *in toto*, not as erotic opportunities. "You just want me for my body"; how often have we cried that, in our hearts, if not out loud? Masters and Johnson recognized that problems occur for a woman when her "desire for sexual expression crashes into a personal fear that her role as a sexual entity is without the unique contribution of herself as an individual."[7] "I want to be somebody's *somebody*," said Beth, a college senior. "I've had two bad relationships recently. In both I wanted what I was giving: love and emotional commitment; eventually I wanted marriage. I wanted more than anything to have someone to love and love me back, but both times the men backed off, for reasons I've yet to get straight."

We often feel terribly pressured not to admit that we may not *want* to be free. We feel guilty at our inability to be emotionally detached, and trapped by the new rhetoric that permits a woman—whether she likes it or not—to be as sexually adventurous as a man. Here again the women's movement and the sexual revolution clash head-on. As writer Jacqueline Swartz pointed out, "Often the more independent and accomplished a woman is in her job or profession, the more easily she can be conned into feeling guilty about expressing her need to a man, particularly a man who seems to want a 'good soldier' and who encourages the worst kind of 'chin-up,' 'control your feelings' masculine behavior. Let this woman admit to wanting an ongoing relationship and she's in for a massive dose of discomfort."[8]

THE MAN GAP: QUALITY AND QUANTITY

Here I am, an unusual, cultured and attractive 37-year-old woman sitting in my Manhattan apartment wondering where all the stable, cultured, witty, generous and adventurous gentlemen are.

Ad, *New York Review of Books*

I've heard the complaint everywhere, over and over: "There are no good men." A cocktail party in Atlanta was an echo of dozens of other occasions. "There just aren't any interesting, straight, upwardly mobile, capable, non-neurotic men anymore," remarked Tyrania, a Georgia businesswoman who is all that and more. She went on to categorize the men in the room. "Those are the married men," she said, bobbing her wineglass in a tally that included most of the men there. "And now for a count of the quote, eligible men, unquote. He's living with someone, he's gay, he's weird, he's a perennial bachelor." I had to admit to knowing exactly what she meant as we trooped into the dinner table with six other—*terrific*—unattached women.

We're not just hypercritical, it's not sour grapes from the women who don't have men of their own. The Census Bureau tells us that statistically there are *fewer* men. Back in 1910, there

were 106 men for every 100 women, but by 1980 women out-
numbered men 100 to 94.5. For every 100 men over fifteen
who are single—never married, divorced, or widowed—there
are 123 women. Only in the age group 25–29 are there more
unmarried men than women: 100 men for every 88 women.
The lament "A good man is hard to find" is based on cold
scientific truth.

If we break it down further, it's even more depressing. In
the age group 35–39, there are 100 unattached men to 128
unattached women. Between ages 40 and 44, men get thirty-
five more available women per hundred; and between 45 and
55, the figures leap—100 men get their pick of 147 women in
their age group. The imbalance is compounded by the fact that
men on the average marry women 2.3 years younger than
they, and while 83 percent of divorced men remarry, only 75
percent of divorced women do.[9]

Ironically, our very success in the last fifteen years or so has
contributed substantially to our discomfort by creating a quality gap that compounds the quantity gap. William Novak, author of The Great Man Shortage, ascribes the gap to women's
overall emotional growth—through consciousness raising,
therapy, and our growing tendency to talk among ourselves.
We have far outstripped men, who, with the exception of a
few tiny clusters around the country, have had no comparable
men's movement. Some of us have achieved positions equal
to men's in the work world, and more of us are trying. But a
woman who delays marriage to become successful may well
find upon reaching her goal that there are few eligible men
who can match her status.

Men today, for women past their late twenties, are often
disappointing as people. "They might be successful in their
careers, but in terms of human relationships they seem to be
lacking something. They are often unable to tolerate intimacy
and commitment (which a woman can find, at the very least,
among her female friends)."[10] It's likely that a man who is her
equal is eyeing that ever-increasing pool of younger women

for his mate. A woman who is a high achiever would do well to stand back and ask herself if she is still looking for a man who is "better" than she: richer, smarter, older, more powerful. We're used to "marrying up" under the terms of the old marriage contract. As we gain in status and power, not only is it no longer necessary, it's impossible. "We're so equal now," one woman told me bitterly, "that we're *better*. And I still can't get what I want: an emotionally committed relationship." Rather than retreat, it behooves us to encourage men to grow to meet us.

Men tend to treat women in terms of a mistaken belief about feminism: "separate but equal" seems to be the ideology that men think women approve.[11] While he's conscientiously splitting all the checks down to the penny and *not* opening the door, she's trying to figure out how to create a new standard for a relationship. We no longer care who lights our cigarettes; we care about the quality of our lives, and the desire to share them with some interesting caring man.

TECHNIQUE VERSUS TENDERNESS

There's an abyss the size of the Grand Canyon between my lovemaking and the techniques in the new "how to drive a man sexually wild" books. The sexual revolution gave me a lot of freedom, but it didn't make me a freer person. I can sleep with anyone I want to whenever I want to, but I'm not freer with my body. I still find it hard to tell a man what I want, or need or like in bed.

Lisa, 25

We're subject to a particularly contemporary anxiety: whether we'll get high marks for our sexual performance. In an era of quantifiable response—sex flush, heightened breathing rate, hand clutch—sex can seem mechanical, a skill rather than an emotional exchange. Having sex is like driving a car:

it might break down on you, and if so, "how to" and "fix it" manuals abound.

The most recent "discovery" in the world of human response has been the G-spot, which when stimulated is said to produce a deep uterine orgasm and ejaculation in some women.[12] It can be quite threatening. "First we had to contend with 'Did you come?' Then it was 'Did you come twice?' And now it's 'Did you spurt?' " said Sandra, a sex educator, when we discussed the latest performance standard women may be expected to meet.

Philip and Lorna Sarrel, in their book *Sexual Unfolding*, talk about the old tyranny of the "thou shalt nots" being replaced by the new despotism of the "thou shalts": "Thou shalt have and enjoy multiple orgasms and enjoy an active sex life . . . [which] cause just as much misery and harm as sexual repression."[13] The new expectations objectify and dehumanize a woman just as successfully as the old "don'ts" that Good Girls hear. We've progressed from virtue to virtuosity, but it doesn't make us happy. "I can't stand all of the 'do this, do that, touch here, don't touch there' stuff," said a woman working toward her doctoral degree at a university where I was teaching. "Sex isn't supposed to be a talkathon, it should be natural. I hate it when a man expects me to be a sexual expert." It's particularly difficult for a Good Girl, taught by word and example not to be sexual, to deal with this new sexual expertise. "I want sex to be sensual, not scientific," an up-and-coming graphic artist told me. "I like the satin sheets approach to sex."

In some ways we are the first generation of sexually obligated women in America—obligated to be sexually fulfilled. Among the seemingly endless contradictory expectations of modern women, sexual expertise is not the least. Nathaniel Wagner, the late sex researcher, struck a cautionary note: "We obtained information about the effects on the heart of walking on the moon before we obtained information about the effects upon the heart of sexual behavior in the bedroom. Obviously, our skills in telemetry are not the problem."[14] Our skills in matters of the heart—or lack of them—may well be.

THE BACKLASH: SEXUAL REVISIONISM

There was a time in my early twenties when I had sex quite frequently and with a lot of different men. I thought it was great; all of this opportunity to express myself sexually. But after a while, frankly, I began to find it boring. I'd rather not meet a man or date a man just for sex. You have to stand back and see that a couple of hours of pleasure aren't worth the position you sometimes find yourself in.

Louise, 36

Revisionism is in the air. Out of the 106,000 respondents to *Cosmopolitan's* poll, author Linda Wolfe discovered that more than half were disappointed and disillusioned with the sexual revolution. "The feeling that sexual freedom had benefited men more than women was a predominant underlying complaint. . . . Close to 50 percent of the women believe that sex today had become too casual and too difficult to avoid, and that they themselves, and perhaps all women, had become pawns in a revolution engineered chiefly by men."[15] This wouldn't be so significant if the women who participated in the poll were prudish or inexperienced, but she describes them as perhaps the most sexually comfortable and experimental group of women in Western history. The majority had had numerous sexual partners, and most had participated in a considerable variety of sexual practices. But discontent is still abundant. There's no vision of a sexual utopia here. This woman's description of her ambiguity speaks for many of us:

I partly enjoy the benefits of the sexual revolution. I feel I'm freer to make my own decisions about sex instead of having them already made for me. On the other hand, too much freedom can be a difficult thing to handle. And the results of my own decisions are not always positive; they can be detrimental.

The freedom has sometimes proved oppressive: the key advantage of the new order, overwhelming possibility, is also its key disadvantage. We still aren't sure of the rules—are we Good Girls, Bad Girls, or, as we suspect, something still in between? We sense the risk of choosing a course of action that may offer temporary satisfaction but destroy a more valuable part of life. A sexual fling could permanently alienate someone we love. A refusal to have sex can dead-end a relationship.

In a political debacle that seemed to echo the private chaos that women are experiencing, the ERA was defeated in the summer of 1982. To some, it was an added suspicion to the growing concern that the sexual revolution was simply a rip-off, another example of the masculine world taking advantage of and oppressing the feminine. "Women regard men as usurpers of power, as denying their rights and status," wrote George Bach in his article "Caring." "Men resent women encroaching on their territory and feel threatened by the upheaval of the old order. So polarized are the sexes that rational dialogue and interaction are sometimes impossible." [16]

The majority of American women want a loving, stable, and committed relationship with a man; but it seems that men want something else, and we don't know the methods to get what *we* want. And we wonder, what now?

7

ROMANCE—RENAISSANCE OR REGRESSION?

THE NEW CHARLIE

"Charlie"—Revlon's signature woman in its ads for the perfume of that name—was portrayed by actress Shelley Hack. Long and lean, she was the quintessential liberated woman: single, employed, casually chic in functional but elegant pants and man-tailored jacket. She went to bars unescorted, signed the check in restaurants, walked with a loose and confident stride, arms swinging. Independent, strong, and sexy in her self-satisfaction.

Enter the new Charlie. Revlon replaced Hack this year with a softer, rounder model. The pants are gone; in their place is a ruffled strapless evening gown. *And she's with a man*, a handsome, wholesome-looking young professional—a banker, a lawyer? The romantic scene is set as Charlie and her date walk home from a party. "Would you cancel your trip to the coast if I proposed?" he asks, and Charlie ignores him. But he persists. "Even my mother thinks it's time for you to settle down." Sweetly smiling, Charlie finally looks him straight in the eye and says, "Your mother is right."

We don't know if she skipped her trip, and we don't know if she married her ardent suitor, but one thing is obvious: she didn't look him straight in the eye and say, "Your mother is *wrong.*"

This about-face was no accident. Revlon has been modifying its ad campaign little by little over the years to stay, as executive vice president for advertising Stanford Buchsbaum says, "at the leading edge of where people's emotions, psyches, and intellects have been going. Charlie hasn't changed, the world has changed."[1]

Market research by Yankelovich, Skelly and White, a leading reporter of cultural trends, indicates that there is more interest now in traditional relationships, in marriage, in families. A 1980 poll they conducted found that nearly 96 percent of the people interviewed were dedicated to the ideal of a couple sharing a life and home together in monogamy.[2] (A recent NBC/AP poll had more cynical findings: 60 percent of the people queried did not think that most couples getting married expect to remain married for the rest of their lives. Our hopes and dreams sometimes collide head-on with our perception of reality.)

Love is in the air; we're regressing to the old romantic ideals of love and marriage. Many of us used to think it was a sellout to want a stable monogamous relationship, but the message that marriage equals status, security, and happiness for a woman has resurfaced. Young women who talk about career plans and independence admit that there had better be a man in the background who wants marriage, too, or they feel enormous anxiety.[3]

Ten years or so ago, motherhood was considered to be on the way out. A woman with children was not only an object of pity, burdened as she was with overwhelming responsibilities, but viewed with some disdain because she could have avoided the whole mess. Career women now seem concerned about the possibility of motherhood. Many unmarried women in their thirties are agonizing over the fact that they might not have children. Sometimes it is not so much that they want the responsibility of being a mother, but that they worry their lives will be devoid of a great womanly experience. Under the surface of change, many of the old ideas of how a woman can achieve fulfillment are alive and well.

College students are now mentioning careers, marriage, and children in their future; five years ago they only projected careers as their goal. In fact, in one survey only 45 percent of working women in 1980 felt that their jobs were indeed part of their lifelong plans. A traditional marriage with the male as the sole source of support was the goal for 42 percent of these women.[4] The years roll by and not much changes. As a recent report points out: For most women, marriage ranks higher than a career as a lifetime goal.

In a poll at Brown University, a slight majority (57 percent) of the three thousand co-eds queried felt that when children were under two years old, mothers shouldn't work.[5] Fifty-two percent approved of women taking full-time jobs after their children were older than six. Obviously, the working role of a woman was seen as a choice, and further assumed a financially secure man who could support a family. It all smacks of the old stereotypes of the proper place for a woman: relegated to home and hearth, financially dependent and subservient once again.

The truth is: *we never gave up hoping that Mr. Right would come and sweep us away from all of this.* Women simply don't have a satisfactory substitute fantasy. Rarely do we dream about running a large corporation or making a killing in the stock market. The career woman is a ubiquitous fixture in the national media, but we know that most women's jobs are not for fun, and for little profit. Linda Blocki comments, "A problem women are having is that there are these areas in our lives that need magic, we need to feel swept off our feet. Sometimes it feels so nice to say 'come and control me, tell me where we are going out to dinner, order wonderful food and delicious wine.' " Andrea, a thirty-seven-year-old divorced mother of two, put it this way: "I sometimes lose my head, not utilizing my judgment or good sense. I allow someone else to lead so I don't have to be in charge. Being in charge grows heavy."

Writer Colette Dowling discovered that this deep wish to be taken care of keeps women in a half-light, retreating from the full use of their minds and creativity. She calls this the "Cinderella complex" and says, "Like Cinderella, women today are still waiting for something external to transform their lives."[6] And all signs of this something external, as I see it, point to love. Since we wore our first pair of patent-leather Mary Janes, we have been told that love is the key to the meaning of life, that nothing else matters.

LOVE JUNKIES

All Good Girls were taught to be love junkies; we learned to place a premium on the attainment of love. Never mind that love, through most of history, had nothing to do with marriage, or was a lucky side effect. Never mind that romance for centuries has been the sweetener—artificial at that—of a woman's virtual serfdom within a monogamous relationship. Never mind that a woman whose energies are directed at an ephemeral emotional goal is much less likely to direct those energies toward á concrete one, like a management position in a large corporation. The thrill of being Swept Away—and it is a thrill—has bound us to our history.

Barbara Lazear Ascher points out some love-junkie attributes: "We were, after all, taught to wish upon a star, pluck petals from daisies to determine the murmurs of our hearts, wait for fairy godmothers and the brief wave of the magic wand. Our earliest heroines reinforced these lessons. Cinderella's masochistic goodness was rewarded by the magic delivery of a no-strings-attached coach and coachman, an independently wealthy husband and happily-ever-after. Snow White's stupidity resulted in rescue. All she had to do was lie there and wait. And Rapunzel, empty-headed with a beautiful

head of hair, relied on that hair to end her trials and tribula-
tions. All of these soft, milky, red-cheeked maidens emitting
their Walt Disney glow sent us the same message: Be very
good and very still and your wishes will come true."[7]

Love junkies are passive, the perfect victims to be Swept
Away. We learned we'd get a prince and a kingdom (Rose
Red, who wanted more, was rewarded with toads who leapt
out of her mouth when she spoke up to ask for more) and so
we learned to wait, to hold out for Mr. Right, the purveyor of
these romances. The handsome stranger who would rescue us
from the powerless asexuality of childhood and sweep us into
tumultuous, passionate womanhood. As harmless as it seems,
this yearning for romance has informed our unconscious for
so long and shaped the way we see ourselves so powerfully,
that we still view our lives through a glass, darkly—through
the medium of our men.

We are love needy. Woman are forever in thrall to the language of love. We crave it, we're addicted. Even when we
hear those magic words "I love you," we want more, we want
to hear it again and again. I'm always amazed when, during a
quiet evening spent reading in bed with my husband Bob—he
with the latest political analysis, me with something about sex
research—I turn to him, completely out of the blue, to get his
attention. "Yes," he says, without batting an eyelash. "Yes, I
do love you." How did he know; is my need so apparent? I
was unconscious of my own need until it was vocalized.

But we can't get enough assurance—in the middle of the
night, in the middle of dinner, no matter where; I have yet to
meet a woman who finds an inappropriate time for the declaration of love. And this dependency is not like an addiction, it
is an addiction. Lord Byron said it: "Man's love is of man's life
a thing apart. 'Tis woman's whole existence." Even if we dis-
agree, those exalted emotions when we think we've found Mr.
Right, and our abject misery when he turns out to be Mr.
Wrong, reveal a certain truth to his words.

We think that we can *will* love: if we simply love a man hard enough, long enough, it is inevitable that we'll earn his love through this devotion. We tell ourselves that if we can conjure up romance hard enough we will *both* fall in love. We wish upon a star . . . upon anything . . . Make this experience be as much to him as it is to me . . . something lasting . . . something magical . . . *Please* make it work out this time . . .

This is really an objectifying tactic, disguising the real person in our fervent push for the dream of romance. And rejection infuriates—and scares—us because we've been taught that love is our birthright. How often in a new relationship have you wondered "Is this love?" rather than "What's he like?" The value of simply having a relationship is possibly exceeding the value of the person himself, and this is sure to lead to disappointment.

When being in charge of our lives grows heavy, we still seek to sugarcoat the pill by concentrating on rescue by some special, wonderful man. We speak of finding love, falling in love. We exist in a constant state of tension: will we ever have the Real Thing? We've learned that we can be strong, independent, self-sufficient. But it's a struggle; we're new at it and when the choices seem too confusing, or the path too stony, our dreams of escape reflect a nostalgia for what seemed to be more clear-cut choices. We regress to the old ideals of a man, security, romance.

MR. RIGHT

When I do get serious, I want the man to be ten or fifteen years older than me, tall, dark, handsome and erotic—maybe a foreigner.

Cornelia, 18

We begin the dream early on: the search for Mr. Right, he who is smarter, taller, richer. We scribble his name and ours on notebooks in grammar school, entwine initials in public places, chant "he loves me, he loves me not" as we determine our future on the fall of a petal, intone "love, hate, courtship, marriage" over elaborate pairing of names to predict the man of our dreams.

Even as children, we drift off into plotting life based upon a romantic story line. Teenage romances contain all the same ingredients and messages as their adult counterparts, although they're squeaky clean and wholesome in the first-kiss, will-he-ask-me-to-the-prom genre. Journalist Christine Madsen found that the heroines "all want a boyfriend who is invariably a year or so older, strong, and conventionally handsome. The plots are either predictable or contrived. The girl always ends up with the boy of her dreams or someone even better."[8]

When I asked women about their fantasies as little girls, about the roles they saw themselves in when they grew up, the overwhelming response had to do with marriage—and not simply marriage, but with the actual ceremony itself. Men as boys dreamed fire engines and police chases; women dreamed the number of bridesmaids and the color of their dresses.

An anonymous respondent spun her fantasy for me: "We have a whirlwind courtship, followed by an outrageously beautiful wedding at the Beverly Hills Hilton. *And* I discover he isn't really a humble camera technician but the son of the owner of a world-wide camera manufacturer. We go to France and live happily ever after in his family's castle." Fantasy may reflect the things we know we can never achieve, but it also reflects the things we desire. And we still desire romance: we're willing to trade all we might be for stars in our eyes.

Bridal merchants, those purveyors of white stretch limousines, wedding cancellation insurance, and receptions that cost $10,000 for five hours (for a memory meant to last a lifetime), are members of a burgeoning profession.

These new ceremonies are definitely fantasy material: accouterments range from mobile discotheques to videotapes of the ceremony, from the classic filmy negligees of the bride's trousseau to memory candles with the wedding invitation and a photograph of the happy couple embedded in wax. In the last five years the sale of hope chests has soared. One bride-to-be explained the excess: "You get so tired of scrimping on everything these days. For one day in your life you want to be Queen for a Day."[9] The culmination of Swept Away, and a return to the traditional values and desires of the Good Girl.

Germaine Greer discusses the myth of Mr. Right: "[It's] still as widely dispersed as it ever was, although permissiveness is loudly argued to have made great inroads upon it. It has no demonstrable relation to what actually happens in the majority of cases, but this fact itself reflects nothing upon its sway as a myth. The myth has always depended upon the richness, the handsomeness, the loverliness, the considerateness of a man in a million."[10] The male-female ratio *is* definitely skewed against a woman; when it's skewed by emotion as well as plain hard figures, when we hope that we'll win the one right man out of the million or so wrong ones, when we believe there *is* such an animal, it bears the same relation to actuality as hoping to win the daily double on a bet made because of complementary colors on the jockey's silks. Women can—and do— make their entire lives unhappy and unfulfilled because of this insistence on the perfect Slayer of Dragons, the one-and-only rescuer.

CLAY FEET

Since I was a young girl, I imagined I would marry a doctor who is about five foot eleven, with dark hair and blue eyes. He will like soft jazz, good food and wine, have a sense of humor and be very sexy.

Kate, 37

Linda Blocki comments: "I'm beginning to see an old-fashioned pattern. I see women saying what they need in a man the same way they make out a grocery list: I need a man who is sensitive, someone who likes to take hikes, someone who loves theater, old movies, bluesy songs. Women say 'I never date a man who isn't at least six feet tall' or 'I would never date a blond man. I'm only interested in a man with dark hair.' "

Kate's shopping list is amazingly specific, but there's no room for a flesh-and-blood human in her ideal. It's unlikely that any one man will have all those attributes. The result: disappointment, disillusionment. Attempts to force the wrong man into her preconceived ideals; inability to recognize a compatible lover because of Mr. Right "blindness."

We set our sights so high for so long that to look across the table at a man who isn't perfect doesn't fulfill the fantasy. So we do one of two things: we search again for a man closer to our mental image, or we overlay characteristics on the man we do have to make him conform to our romantic ideal. We literally put together his personality as if we were casting the lead in a play we wrote.

"I know Bill has a lot to say," was a comment by a woman trying to tell me why she married her husband. "But he's very shy. I know he can go far in the company he works for if he puts his mind to it. I had hoped he would be promoted by now, but I'm sure it will happen in the very near future. He really is smart and charming, it just takes a while to appreciate him."

Does he have these attributes or not? It isn't possible to say. He does in her mind, at least for now. But if we don't take a clear-eyed look at this man of our dreams, we succumb to our own fantasy. The first flush of sexual desire successfully hides feet of clay—but when that glow fades, and a woman is faced with a man who leaves the top off the toothpaste or who doesn't like Brahms, or in some other way doesn't fit her shopping list, too often she falls back on her dreams and, inflexible and disappointed, she drives the man away by dwelling on his imperfections or ends the relationship herself, telling herself sadly that the man "was not what he seemed to be."

Janet's experiences are an example. "I keep repeating a pattern. When I meet a man I think is special, we start talking, tell each other all sorts of things. We couldn't have more in common—we tell jokes, laugh, make love, stay up until dawn —and I never see him again. I'm not a casual person about sex, so how do I get into these one-night stands? It never feels casual; it always feels like the real thing." In this case the "real thing" was shared jokes, twelve or fourteen hours in each other's company, and sexual intercourse. Hardly the things one would rationally want to base an entire life's relationship on. Janet was tricked by a fantasy: rather than accepting the pleasure of the experience, she demanded something of it that simply wasn't there. That raw material she thought she could mold resisted her vision of himself as tender, committed mate. He had a mind of his own, a fantasy that didn't jibe with hers. She found out, time and again, that the drama that is Swept Away is really only a one-woman show.

Joyce, a secretary in her forties, was unusually clear-eyed if cynical about the process. "Unfortunately, most men and women do not have clear, conscious ideas about what they are looking for in a relationship. They are not aware of their own programming. Often that programming is spurious, absurd relative to real need, but it's wrapped up with glamour. Glamour? That's when the value of the wrapping exceeds the value of the contents."

DOLLARS FOR DESIRES

The media, wizards of marketing and always quick to scent a weakness in the buying public, push this need for fantasy. They know that desire plus dreams equals cold hard cash. The newest cigarette—an object that is fundamentally unattractive, addictive, life-destroying, and consequently very *unro-*

mantic—has been given a smooth satiny slinky image and advertised with all the silky come-on and romantic appeal of a negligee commercial. Saturday night, the loneliest night of the week for those at home by themselves, offers a substitute for a mate, a romantic fix of classic movies and girl meets boy, fairy tales that feed directly into the veins of the love junkie.

Jan Hoffman discovered an interesting side effect of the Romantic Renaissance: women are wearing more makeup. Cosmetics sales have risen approximately 10 percent a year in the last decade. She quotes Amy Green, entrepreneur of Bendel's Beauty Checkers, a cosmetics make-over emporium: "Women are forever hopeful . . . We are each products of great expectations, and we carry something of that dream around with us our entire lives. I give women hope." And a young saleswoman Hoffman interviewed spoke about her generation's return to romance, explaining, "See, in the beginning, in the '50s, women had to stay home and look pretty. They got so bored that they fought it all out in the '60s. But by the mid-'70s they went too far. They were looking and acting just like men, and so men stopped treating them as feminine. Stopped opening doors and stuff. That's why, wherever you look now, women are back to wearing makeup and sexy dresses. Hopefully now, things'll go back more to the way we were."

"Makeup is emblematic," says Hoffman. "Women are again thinking of beauty as a way to appeal to employers, employees, friends, and lovers. Beauty is a traditional and certainly accepted mode for women to be powerful—though the power may actually be only as substantial as powdered blusher."[11]

We cover our nagging, inner uncertainties with those outer layers of creams, powders, lipsticks, and glossers, a throwback to the times when we knew our place in the world was secured by our skills at capturing a man who would keep us safely tucked away, visible mainly in the kitchen and the bedroom. Our new forays into the boardroom induce the panic of navigating uncharted shores, and we fall back on what we know:

our power to seduce. Floudering for a definition of ourselves, we're particularly susceptible to media manipulation. The title of a recent book tells the tale: *The Moving Target: What Every Marketer Should Know About Women.*[12]

ROMANTIC FICTIONS

Publishing houses are as savvy at big business and big bucks as Revlon and Lorillard. *Publisher's Weekly,* the trade journal to the industry, recently devoted an entire special Valentine's Day issue to that phenomenal money-maker, the romance novel. It's a natural, a direct trade-in on women's dreams for dollars. Twenty million readers (mostly women) spend over $200 million annually on those slender tomes that contain and codify the Swept Away formula.[13] Their structure is as rigid as church litany. Some guidelines given to the would-be romance writer:

> We are looking for a contemporary novel where the romance and sexual relationship between the heroine and hero grow believably out of shared experiences, feelings, and a loving commitment, leading to marriage. The heroine is always young (19 to 27). Often she is starting a career, leaving college, unhappy with her present job or too caught up in her work.
>
> The hero is eight to twelve years older than the heroine. He is self-assured, masterful, hot-tempered, capable of violence, passion, and tenderness . . . rich and successful in the vocation of his choice. He is always tall, muscular (but not muscle-bound) and above all virile.
>
> The heroine's feelings and thoughts should be related to the reader (though not agonizingly or at length), as well as her physical response to the hero.
>
> Sex can be fairly explicit without being too graphic. It should be in good taste and should focus on the sensuous rather than the sexual; the love bond should be stronger than the physical.

Bringing them to the brink of consummation and then forcing them to retreat either because of an interruption or because one or both of the lovers suffer from doubt or shame is an appropriate dramatic device. Above all, your love scenes should be romantic—our readers should be in love with the hero as is the heroine.[14]

It's as if, in the pages of these slender novels, we can let go of all the confusing, sometimes painful stresses of our lives as liberated women. Here Good is Good, Bad is Bad, and the woman *always* gets her man in the generic fantasy that is standard Swept Away fare of the happy woman "gliding toward mother-of-pearl sunsets under the protective arm of a well-muscled, well-heeled viscount whose lips—passionate and demanding—can make heaven rain rose petals, send choirs of angels into glorious song and induce cardiac bliss."[15]

A breakdown of readers by a marketing survey indicates that the average reader is in her early thirties, is married, works, and has some college education. Many readers buy as many as thirty volumes a month. Marriage counselor Dr. Emery Breitner suggests that Freud's oft-repeated query—"What do women want?"—might well be answered if more men read and paid attention to romances. "They would discover that romantic love and courtship are what most women seek and desire, and by fulfilling this need first, the relationship can be even more rewarding for the man."[16] In some way, most of us are still Good Girls who, deep down, want Mr. Right to approve of us and adore us.

The degree of sophistication in selling these romances reflects the enormous economic impact they have on the publishing industry. Imprint names are blatantly romantic—Candlelight Ecstasy Romance, Second Chance at Love (for widows and divorcees specifically), Harlequin Romances, Coventry Romances. Even the cover art is carefully designed for its psychological impact. The borders within borders reflect the ultimately safe, stable, rigidly formulaic world of romance fiction.

February 14. Valentine's Day to the romantic. Cool cash day to the publishers of romance fiction, marked by these publicity events:

Harlequin Books gives a party for 250 of New York's most romantic women—the readers of romance fiction. Editor-in-Chief Fred Kerner tosses a bridal bouquet to the throng.

Pocket Books celebrates by inaugurating Follow Your Heart Romances, an imprint for girls ten and up, with *Cupid Computer* as the first title.

Avon's publicity department issues T-shirts for men bearing the legend (and I use the word advisedly) "Mr. Right." For women, "I found Mr. Right." Both to publicize Avon's new romance line, Finding Mr. Right.[17]

Other seasonal titles that fed the love junkies' romance hunger included *Displays of Affection, How to Kiss with Confidence,* and *Your Wedding.* The ultimate how-to recently hit the market: *How to Get Married.*

The tremendous success of the modern fairy-tale movie *An Officer and a Gentleman* stunned cynics in the accounting departments of the motion picture industry. The poor-girl-gets-upwardly-mobile-boy fable, with a finale where he literally sweeps her off her feet and out of the paper mill where she works, is simply an update—and affirmation—of our penchant for storybook solutions, of Mr. Right to the rescue. It manipulated the heartstrings and pocketbooks of the entire country. Including mine.

"What's funny," said Taylor Hackford, the director, in an interview with critic Gene Siskel, "is that when it came time to actually set up to film the scene in the Tacoma paper mill, about twenty women workers were standing around kibbitzing. But when they saw the rehearsal where Richard [Gere] kisses Debra [Winger] . . . they just broke up and some started crying and others were just applauding. . . . Based on what I saw in that reaction to the rehearsal, I decided to keep that ending."[18]

That scene obviously struck a powerful chord. Even knowing it was make-believe was not enough to deprive those watching women of their identification with the myth: they responded to their *own* myths and dreams as much as to the movie's reinforcement of their fantasies.

7-ELEVEN INTIMACY

I think, to continue Barbara Lazear Ascher's fairy-tale analogy, that I must sound like one of Snow White's cohorts: Grumpy, the dwarf, with my dire warnings: romance is bad, women make fools of themselves in the quest of a nonexistent prince.

I *don't* think love is bad, or wrong or confining. I *do* think our inability to separate the myth of love from the reality is damaging because it results in behavior that hurts us. Listen to Donna: "I just can't tell the real thing from the phony. I tell myself to hold on, not to fall in love with just anyone who comes along. But damn, I meet a guy who seems to me a cut above and before you know it I feel—what? It sure feels like love, or like falling in love. So we spend a little time together, and then—like Puff the Magic Dragon—he's gone and I feel like a teenage dope. What's that song—'I Learned the Truth at Seventeen'? Well, I'm still trying to learn some truth about love, and I'm thirty!"

Kay, thirty-three, has a similar history. "By the time I was eighteen or nineteen, I had no moral qualms about having intercourse as long as I was 'in love.' After my divorce two years ago, I became part of the singles' world again and thought, WOW! Sex! But I just keep falling in love on the first date. I love to be in love, but most of the time there isn't a second date."

Love that is real is a developing emotion, slow and steady. It means caring for another person, clay feet and all. It's a compassion for another's fears and problems, a willingness to invest time and effort in developing the potential of a relationship.

Unfortunately, when we are in a constant search for the "perfect" relationship, we don't seem to understand that it requires time, work, effort. As soon as a new man appears on our horizon we want to define and test the limit of the relationship rather than learn its endurance. Deborah Hughes Morningstar's shrewd insight struck me:

Whether it be food, sex, twenty-four-hour banking or fast photos, we no longer believe that waiting is part of the excitement, part of the pleasure. If we want Doritos at one o'clock in the morning, we can run into any convenience store and get them. The same applies to sex. We know that if we go to a bar, most of us can find a sexual partner. It may take four hours—it used to take months, money, commitment, and marriage. We have been spoiled by the immediacy offered and expected in our society. We want it *all* and we want it *now*.

8

GOOD GIRLS AND BAD CONTRACEPTION

RISK FOR ROMANCE

I was in Alexandria, Louisiana, in the fall of 1975, working on a continuing education program with the Louisiana Family Planning Project. Outlining factors involved in contraceptive motivation on a chalkboard and emphasizing how erratic and inconsistent teenagers are about using birth control, I was suddenly struck by an emotional flashback that had the force of a blow.

I saw myself at twenty-one; I felt the coolness of the sink pressing against my forehead as I sat on the edge of the tub in the bathroom of the tiny first house my husband and I rented. Day after day I sat resting my head against the white porcelain as I listened to the water dripping from the faucet. And I, though not religious, prayed fervently that I wasn't pregnant. I remember bargaining out loud, my voice echoing in the tiled space, "Dear God, if you let me get by just this once, I promise, I absolutely swear, I'll never take another chance." The floor of that bathroom is still clear to me today: little white hexagons with blue squares interspersed, a geometric sea of white daisies with blue eyes. I sat there for hours on end, immobilized by anxiety and dread. Sometimes I stood up, leaned my hands on the sink, and looked at myself in the mirror, pleading with the powers that be that it was "just a lousy mistake, so don't let me be pregnant." I can still feel that same sick, trapped reaction I had back then. Menstruation reprieved me after a long, long week, but the memory of how it feels to sweat out a period has never left me.

I interrupted my lecture to describe my own experience with birth control. There were some twenty women in that room, most of whom I knew only casually. We'd never exchanged intimacies before, but as I talked we subtly grew together, a group with a shared traumatic experience, those "Dear God, don't let me be pregnant" moments in our lives. Every woman there had a similar tale: scare story after scare story tumbled out. Fascinated and appalled, I began to investigate the phenomenon of the bad contraceptor.

"How many of you have ever had unprotected intercourse —sex without some form of birth control—when you were not planning pregnancy?" A simple question; I asked it of 125 women from all over the country who were attending a workshop on human sexuality. I expected lapses, but the response astonished me. Every woman in the room raised her hand. Why? I asked them. Why? The answers I got were echoed by women across the country; they reverberated back into my own girlhood. *"Romance,"* they told me. *"Spontaneity."* "There is nothing more awful than premeditated sex." "Planning takes away all the romance; I need to be seduced to enjoy sex." One hundred and twenty-five women were willing to risk unwanted pregnancy for an ephemeral need to be Swept Away. And so was I.

Those women and I were all professionals in the field of family planning, a field that has traditionally demanded women's right to control their bodies through controlling reproduction. We were an educated, motivated bunch. The Pill had been around for ten years, we all knew the ins and outs of every other form of birth control as well. We were constantly surrounded with talk of birth control, with supplies, books, movies on the topic. Sex without fear of pregnancy was within our grasp, and we—to a woman—had shirked responsibility, a responsibility most of us had been crusading for long and vigorously.

It goes on and on. I began informally to ask my students at the University of New Mexico if they had ever taken risks. Almost all had; some only the first few times they had sex, when they were in their teens, others much more often. On hundreds of occasions at workshops across the country, I've raised the issue, and the outcome is always the same. There are never more than a very few women who always use contraception, most often younger women. As the confessions come pouring forth in incredible number, the response is astonishment; few can believe they are members of such a numerous—and foolish—sorority.

When I reflect on this gap between availability and use of birth control, I think back to my work at Planned Parenthood, particularly on the days when we had pregnancy testing, and the kids who should have come to us *before* for help came, all too often, too late to prevent pregnancy. Those days were always difficult. From the window of my office I would watch a scene made heartbreaking by its unnecessary repetition. In cars parked up and down the street, young boys sat, staring and waiting. Out came the girls, getting into the car, sliding over next to their boyfriend, telling the bad news: the test was positive. Then, inevitably, tears and sometimes angry recriminations.

It was saddening to see, maddening to watch so many teenagers come into the clinic. Many of them had been sexually active for up to a year without using contraception. Yet when the test results came back positive, their reactions had a monotonous sameness: "I just didn't think it would happen to me," they moaned. And almost invariably, "I didn't expect to, mean to, go all the way." "He turned me on." "One thing just led to another." It was troubling, it was baffling. The girls knew where to come, how to seek information and help: there they were, by the hundreds, at the clinic. But why had they waited until after intercourse? *Why were all those young women pregnant when they could easily have protected themselves?*

EFFECTIVENESS RATES

The world has spun a lot since the 1950s when the best method of birth control was a condom and a prayer. Today clinics offer a full range of preventive devices, drugstores have enormous sections of simple, over-the-counter methods, information on contraception abounds. But consider these recent statistics: annually there have been 1.5 million abortions performed in America; 11 percent of teenage girls get pregnant every year; more than half the pregnancies of women between the ages of twenty-two and forty-four are unintended; 33 percent of pregnancies *in marriage* are unplanned.[1] I'm not saying that women who are conscientious about using birth control don't have failures inherent in the methods themselves. But let's compare statistics for failure rates if the method is used properly and consistently with those dismal statistics above: oral contraceptives, .34 percent; IUD's, 1–2 percent; condoms, 3–4 percent; foam, 3–4 percent; diaphragms, 3–4 percent.

These failure rates reflect flaws in the actual methods themselves. Human error—improper or inconsistent use of a method—at least doubles the statistical margin for failure in most cases: oral contraceptives, 3 percent; IUD's, 6 percent; condoms, 12 percent; spermicides (foam, etc.), 17.9 percent; sponges, 18 percent; diaphragms, 18.6 percent. For women under twenty-five, the diaphragm failure rate soars to 23.7 percent.[2]

That final dismal statistic may be reflected by another scarifying set of numbers: close to 25 percent of college-age women don't use birth control regularly, even when they are involved in an ongoing relationship. The latest figures indicate that close to 40 percent of unintended pregnancies in women over the age of twenty—that's 1.7 million pregnancies—are the result of failing to use any contraception at all. Some women use a method, then discontinue it. What is very disturbing is how many women appear to get "caught" within a short time of stopping method use. Among a group of women who have had an abortion, 18 percent of prior contraceptive users became pregnant within a month of stopping and 47 percent within three months.[3] The technology of contraception can't protect us if we don't use it.

It has been impossible for me to witness the steady stream of unwanted pregnancies among the clients of birth control clinics, among students I have grown to know, and among my friends and their teenaged daughters without feeling dismay that women are constantly getting themselves into easily preventable situations. Clearly it isn't logical for women to keep on doing this to themselves. What's going on here?

GOOD GIRLS DON'T

When I first had sex, I didn't use birth control because "Nice girls shouldn't have to." To do so would be to face that I was going against strong parental directions. Once I faced my initial guilt over having sex, I felt a strong responsibility to myself not to have an unplanned pregnancy. Since I conquered my guilt I have never had sex without birth control.

Anonymous, 34

We risk unwanted pregnancy, *not* because we don't know about birth control, *not* because we don't know where to get birth control, but *because our ambivalence about our own sexuality leads us to deny that we might need birth control.* Those noes, don'ts, and waits churn around in our minds while our bodies are saying yes, now, do. No matter how knowledgeable we are, no matter how vigilant, almost all of us have risked unwanted pregnancy through poor contraceptive practices.

Contraception carries the same taboos as sex, and like sex, can become emotionally charged, the dumping ground for a woman's negative or ambivalent feelings about her sexuality. Contraception is the cold hard announcement of planned sex. To use birth control effectively, sociologist Kristin Luker found, "you have to acknowledge that you are a sexual person, that you're going to be a sexual person again, and you have to acknowledge that you're planning to have intercourse. You have often to take active and definitive action relative to your partner. You have to do things that are culturally taboo for women in society."[4] When I first read that phrase "culturally taboo" its truth struck me, as I thought of how embarrassed and shy many women are about using contraception.

"One cannot be swept away and prepared at the same time," wrote Pamela Lowry in her 1971 overview of unwanted pregnancy. "For a girl to ask if her partner is 'using something' constitutes clear evidence that she is fully aware of what is about to occur and is participating willingly. For her to use a contraceptive is an admission that she is responsible for her own actions. Avoidance of the reality of her sexuality and its implication is more important to her than communication and action to counter the risk of pregnancy."[5] A Good Girl cannot admit the reality of her sexuality and retain her status: "To be prepared for coitus would give the lie to the rationale that each act of intercourse was unplanned, merely a temporary and transitory lapse of virtue."[6]

Elizabeth Roberts, writing in *Childhood Sexual Learning*, agrees that a young woman faces a dilemma: "She can acknowledge her erotic feelings and run the risk of being identified as promiscuous, or she can live up to the still-popular feminine norms of passivity and non-interest in sex, pretend she was 'swept off her feet' and run the risk of pregnancy."[7] A young surgical nurse had an ingenious solution that satisfied the conditions of being a Good Girl publicly, but kept her protected. "When you are single like I am and you take the Pill, it's just a signal to men that you're available, and frankly,

I don't think men are all that used to women being so available. So what I do is this: even though I'm on the Pill, I pretend that I'm not protected for the first couple of times I have intercourse with a man. That way a man is responsible for the contraception and he has got to use something or we have to postpone having sex. When I get to know him better, I can 'go on the Pill.' I know it's ridiculous, but I just don't want men to think I sleep around."

INNOCENTS ABROAD

I went out with a man last night. Like a dummy, I went totally unprepared for sex. I wanted to take my diaphragm, but I was afraid that he might think I sleep around. I couldn't tell him to use a rubber, it sounded like I'm a little too hip about sex.

Anonymous, 38

Too hip? The woman who told me this is an educator in the field of human sexuality.

It is clear to me that one strong reason women continue to get pregnant when they don't want to be, when they know about contraception, and when methods are readily available, is our training as Good Girls. The terrible trio, ambivalence, anxiety, and vulnerability about our sexual selves, keeps us off-balance. We want—emotionally and physiologically—to have sex. We also want to be loved and respected by the men we're involved with. Yet we've been taught that fulfilling our physical needs deprives us of our love-worthiness. So we waffle, deny the potential for sexual encounters, then indulge unpreparedly and *get pregnant*. Good Girls act like innocents abroad when it comes to protecting themselves.

I rarely meet a man I fall head over heels for at first sight, but there was this guy at a party . . . Funny, I didn't plan on having sex at all. It didn't actually hit me until we were in bed . . . and

I just couldn't say "Excuse me, I gotta put in my diaphragm." I
didn't want him to think I was ready for sex, so I just let myself
get so involved that before I knew it we were making love.

Charlotte, 21

Charlotte was involved in an intimate physical act. Yet to hear
her talk, she was functioning at a level only slightly above
zombie unconsciousness.

For some women, the cost of the explicit admission "I am a
sexual being" is simply too high. Whether to a lover, parent,
doctor, or some abstract moral judge like the teachings of one's
religion, it's very hard for a woman to publicly announce private behavior that might be condemned. And birth control *is*
public. A woman must acknowledge that she is going to have
sex, and she must acknowledge it not only to herself—contra-
vening her internal police—but to a doctor and/or a drugstore
clerk. Depending on her method, an intended partner may
need to be informed. Finally, she must actually use birth control every time she has sex. Pills require at least one recognition a day of sexual intent, IUD's need periodic checking,
diaphragms, condoms, and jelly all demand a physical immediacy.

A special subgroup with contraceptive difficulty is women
who have been advised to stop taking oral contraceptives because of their age, or high blood pressure, or side effects in
combination with smoking. To go from the relatively private
protection of the Pill to the "public" contraception of a barrier
method can reduce even the most seemingly sophisticated
women to adolescent irresponsibility.

I feel as if I'm only posing as a professional in women's health
care. Since I stopped taking the Pill, if I haven't planned ahead
on having sex, I'm as bad a risk-taker as any fifteen-year-old
with braces on her teeth. I feel too embarrassed to stop the
process. I can't bring myself to say "Halt, I have to go into the
bathroom and put in my diaphragm," or "You have a condom,

don't you?" I am sad to admit that I am a good provider of birth control but a poor consumer.

Virginia, mid-30s

A Good Girl simply can't, won't, shouldn't announce, to herself or anyone else, that she is a person with physical desires and longings. So to satisfy her deep duality about sexual matters, she splits off her action, intercourse, from its acknowledgment, contraception.

In her research study of single white women between the ages of eighteen and twenty-three, Pamela Rains discovered that the absence or presence of "moral ambivalence" was the major determinant in the role of effective contraception. When women feel ambivalent and yet have sex, they will be inconsistent about contraception.

Rains suggests that there are four stages involved in a woman's moving from virginity to being comfortable with contraception. "The first stage is falling in love, which provides the rationale for having sex. The second, dating one man exclusively, implies a stable relationship over time. The third involves changing her sexual standard so that she accepts intercourse as *something she is doing herself* rather than depending on seduction by a male to overcome doubts and apprehensions. The fourth is coming to perceive herself as likely to engage in sex in future relationships. While all of these things may occur in various orders or simultaneously, it is the fourth stage that is most likely to produce consistent use of birth control."[8]

GOING PUBLIC

If you think that "going public" about birth control is easy, put yourself in the place of one of my graduate students in a course I team taught with Paul Dearth. The students were preparing to teach in the school system but they needed additional credits to teach sex education. Their assignment: go to a drugstore and buy a method of over-the-counter contraception—women to buy condoms, men to buy foam or jelly. There was a method to this madness: we suspected that the encounter would sensitize them to how delicate a topic contraception can be. "This assignment is totally ridiculous," a woman in her thirties complained, to universal agreement. But everyone came to the next class chagrined at their earlier protestations, and the stories came pouring out. Women talked about feeling flushed and totally exposed. One woman mortified the clerk at the drugstore by going into lengthy and overly loud detail about buying the condoms for class, and not for her personal use. She said the clerk kept trying to ignore her and sidle away, but her embarrassed volubility trapped him.

Another student went to six stores until she found a place where she could buy condoms without asking for them. Even then she picked up a magazine to conceal her package until she got to the cash register, and she waited until the checkout line was totally deserted before she approached.

A third woman asked her date to wait in the car while she ran into the drugstore, not telling him what she was buying. Paralyzed by having to ask an older male pharmacist for help, she waited fifteen minutes until a younger one was free. He waited on her just as her date came in from the car asking, "What happened to you? Can't you find what you want? What's taking so long?" He was shocked, she was mortified, and it took another fifteen minutes of detailed explanation before things got smoothed over.

One of the men reported this unintended double entendre: "Where's the foam?" he asked. "Over there with the other shaving supplies," answered the clerk. The student reported blushing. "No, not that kind of foam, the—um—other kind." The clerk eyed him strangely, then gave him a big wink and said, "Over there," with a leer. Almost everyone agreed that what had seemed to be a simple task had turned out to be a slightly traumatic one. If professional educators feel this ambivalence, multiply it geometrically for the Good Girl buying contraceptives for her own use.

CONTRACEPTION AND THE MEDIA

The golden glow of sunset reflects in the room, the curtain softly billows from the sea breeze, two empty wineglasses sit on the table. Arm in arm, a couple glides upstairs toward romance. The scrolled calligraphy advises: "When the moment becomes more . . . be sure." But read on. "You don't plan it. It just happens. And when it does be sure you have Encare with you . . . you never know what one wonderful moment will lead to . . ."[9] A contraceptive ad that feeds directly into a woman's ambivalence about contraception and that mimics a Good Girl's zombie approach to sex! (I'll give credit though for the advice to use birth control!)

Sex educator Sol Gordon points out, "People say there's all this sex around. What you see on TV is pornography, obscenity, titillation, sadism and sadomasochism; but you don't find sexuality or sex education. From the titillation of suggestion to the blatantly erotic, sex pervades the mass media. But the prudery of prime time's watchdogs means you can't advertise birth control. Birth control is classed with guns, cigarettes and liquor as items not to be advertised on radio and television."[10]

The National Association of Broadcasters surveyed two thousand people to find out how ads for over-the-counter contraceptives would fare on television. The overall reaction was two to one against. Surprisingly, 60 percent of women eighteen to thirty-four years old opposed the ads.[11] Or perhaps less than surprising: Good Girls learn to feel they must bury their sexuality. But certainly sad and disappointing.

BIG, BIG, SIN

When I was growing up, I felt a little guilty when I let my boy-friend touch me above the waist and *really* guilty when I let him cross the magic line below the waist. And I knew you had to be crazy in love to have sex. But the thing you could never do was "plan on it." Using some protection—or making him use a con-dom—was the *worst* thing because it meant you knew you were going to do it and you didn't try and stop yourself.

Sonya, mid-40s

Sonya grew up, as I did, in a family in which religion played a large part in defining proper sexuality. Over the years, my co-worker Angel Martinez and I discovered that women and some men deal with religious and moral strictures against fe-male sexuality and birth control by creating a hierarchy of relative sin. In my own terminology, if petting and necking are a Little Sin, and intercourse is a Big Sin, using birth control is the Big, Big Sin. It's a bold statement that you'd planned to sin all along. James McCary, one of the foremost authorities in the field of human sexuality, discussed sin and contraception: "Many unwanted pregnancies occur among the religiously de-vout, who despite their determination to 'refrain from sin,' somehow lose control and get swept into the act of sexual intercourse. . . . They believe that a purchase [of contracep-tives] made their future sexual relations 'planned sin' which is apparently more damnable than 'unplanned sin.' "[12]

When a woman feels that premarital intercourse is sinful in the eyes of her church or family, she may handle her conflict by conforming to only part of her religious code: "If you are sinning, going against the teachings of the Church, you might as well not make it any worse by being so calculated as to use birth control. One sin at a time. Sex isn't something you can plan on anyway, it's just something that happens." This from a Catholic in her mid-thirties, expressing an attitude that I recognized from my own upbringing in the Catholic Church. You were really bound tight by Mother Church's rulings: premarital sex was a sin, and birth control itself was a sin—not just bad because it showed you planned to have sex, but a *sin*. I feel lingering bitterness toward any religious institution that specifically exalts the procreative function of women to the detriment of all their other capabilities.

Edward Pohlman noted in *The Psychology of Birth Planning* that "to make contraceptive plans is to admit to oneself an intention which, in the thinking of many unmarried individuals, is sinful. To be swept off one's feet when the moon is full requires but a weak moment and can be explained as sudden passion. But planning for contraception may mean that the guilt-ridden individual must live for a long time with the knowledge of his premeditation to sin. The same individual may experience repeated cycles of uncontracepted sex relations, repentance, resolutions never to 'sin' again, and backsliding."[13]

Marian Upchurch's research with four thousand female students ratifies the correlation between guilt and contraceptive difficulties. She found that guilt acted as a psychological barrier to the use of birth control; in some situations women could rationalize sexual activity but not premeditated protection. There was a further corollary between the type of contraceptive and guilt level among women. Condoms were found to be the most guilt-provoking:[14] worse even than acknowledging her own sexuality, a woman whose partner uses a condom believes she is perceived by him as sexual, a sinner, a Bad Girl.

PASSIVE PREGNANCY

"I had my first son because my diaphragm was clear across the room in a drawer and I *knew* it was my safe time." "I can't believe I'm pregnant: I only have unprotected intercourse right around my period." Passive pregnancy: "I didn't know," "I thought I was safe," and a thousand other excuses underline again the lack of involvement we seem to have in decisions about *our own bodies*. There is *never* a safe time for unprotected intercourse: women can conceive while they are menstruating, lactating; some women ovulate *during* intercourse. Because we are often conflicted about contraception, succumbing to seduction removes the burden of decision from our shoulders. "Psychic conflict regarding contraception is to be anticipated as conscious and unconscious reasons for and against its use exist simultaneously. Throughout a larger part of their procreative period, most women are ambivalent about becoming pregnant—an ambivalence which helps them to adjust to monthly uncertainty." [15]

A Good Girl has years of training as a passivist: failing to use contraception is a way of making sure she doesn't have to declare herself sexual, so she drifts into a decision *not* to make a decision.

> I work in a family planning clinic, but I'm almost embarrassed to admit it. I'm seven months pregnant, and we definitely didn't plan this baby at all. In fact, we'd sort of agreed on a childless marriage. We went out on the town last New Year's Eve, and the combination of the champagne, and holiday excitement, and Roy's sexiness—he was really wild and crazy—made me careless and I blew it. When I found out I was pregnant, I was appalled, but now it's not really so bad. I guess deep down I really wanted to have a baby, so maybe forgetting my diaphragm was the best holiday present ever.
>
> *Beth, 29*

NO MORE REGRETS

At twenty-six I got pregnant, had my son, and gave him up for adoption out of the Eddna Gladney Home in Forth Worth, Texas. Although I have not seem him since, I have learned from that experience one very valuable lesson. Decisions affect the rest of our lives; there is no way to have any decision we make end its effect when the immediate results of the decision are finished.

Anne (a counselor), 40

No matter what decision a woman makes about an unintended pregnancy, it bears a price tag. A woman can rehearse in her mind what she would do *if* it happened, but the reality is light-years away from the make-believe. Pregnancy triggers a range of emotions that can be overwhelming and unpredictable, and there is little time to dawdle about with a plan of action. Once pregnant, there isn't a world of options, only three: abortion, delivery and adoption, and delivery and motherhood. Even when the pregnancy is totally unwanted, the decision can be a painful one. It makes a woman feel vulnerable, not in control: angry, anxious, depressed. She can suffer from remorse, become burdened with guilt if her course of action defies religious or family teachings.

A woman can juggle the pros and cons of each option with the man involved, family, friends, go get professional counseling—*but the ultimate decision is hers alone.* It is one of the loneliest decisions a woman ever faces.

A woman never forgets a pregnancy. And this can leave some emotional scars if it wasn't wanted. It can make one distrust men, feel hostile toward them because they *don't* bear the burden of decision. For some women it is an occasional lingering sadness over the whole experience; for others it can be deeper, more damaging. Women who do not have the psychological repertoire to cope with conflict or to make firm decisions are the most vulnerable. They never resolve the experience, but replay it again and again—never satisfied with the choice they made.

I'm not saying that an unwanted pregnancy is a lifetime tragedy; most women deal with the experience and go on. Susan, twenty-nine, talks about how she handled it: "I've had two abortions, one when I was nineteen and the other when I was twenty-two. I was 'sort of' using foam, and told both of the guys not to worry. The first time, I was completely relieved that abortion was legal and available. But the second time, I felt terrible, stupid. It made me take a sharp look at myself. I began to mend my careless fences, and haven't taken a risk since. Not one." A woman can make a creative effort to cope with the pregnancy as a reflective rather than a reflexive process: "The stress of deciding about the outcome can be managed by various strategies of conflict avoidance, reduction, and resolution." [16] But in the end, it's better all around when a woman's pregnancy is an anticipated and joyful event.

CONTRACEPTION: AN ISSUE OF GENDER?

As the old song goes, it takes two to tango. So what about men? Why do they seem to collude with women's contraceptive failings, even when they don't want to be fathers? Men used to be responsible to the "good" women they slept with, and contraception—withdrawal or condoms—was strictly male business. If a woman conceived, the costs to the man were high: possibly a loveless "shotgun" marriage, with attendant curtailment of freedom and the looming specter of eternal support; at the least, the financial and emotional burden of an illegal abortion.

Technological advances in female contraception have relegated men to the role of passive spectator. In 1979, the U.S. Department of Health and Human Services provided only $750,000 for male birth control programs out of a total family planning budget of $242 million. Even that support, paltry as it was, has recently been dropped. And of the $34 million spent in the same year to research new birth control techniques, only 6 percent was devoted to male methods. [17] In 1983 alone, two new female contraceptives were announced: the three-month time-release injection, which has been used in many other parts of the world, and the contraceptive sponge, a new barrier device with an efficacy rate of only 85 percent.[18]

Ironically, the very things that contribute to women's independence—assumption of the responsibility for birth control, the growing belief in "our bodies, ourselves"—have had the unfortunate side effect of reinforcing male distance from the issue of contraception. We certainly didn't count on that happening. Some younger men have never even thought about birth control, and even the older ones may have become so secure that, as Adam, forty-three, said, "I got out of the habit of worrying about getting someone pregnant. In the seventies, you could be pretty sure everyone was on the Pill."

If using contraception proclaims us as sexually active, as cold and pragmatic planners, hard-eyed realists with no romance in our souls, maybe even "on the make," how can it be surprising that it is easier, more delightful, to be Swept Away in a tumult of passion? Being responsible—and thus sexually free—controverts strong cultural ideals that women are sexual only in relationships of duration and commitment. It's a shake-up of the old order, and can be threatening. But it's also one of the most liberating things a woman can do because it's about herself, first and foremost.

9

MEN TALK/MAN TALK

I think sex should be a sharing experience in which two people further express their joy at being together. It should never be the sole basis of a relationship.

I value sex for the way it supports and enriches a love relationship, for the way it unites lovers in a kind of intimacy and shared pleasure. Sex can be an expression of one's attitude of respect and care.

Are you nodding your head in agreement, feeling that two savvy women are expressing more or less what you yourself feel about intimacy, and wondering why men simply don't seem to get it?

Surprise—those two quotes are from a twenty-one-year-old student and a twenty-seven-year-old teacher, both *male*.

As we learn more about the patterns and structures that have shaped us today, it sometimes seems men are the enemy, the oppressors, or at the very least an alien and incomprehensible species. These stereotypes are as destructive as the ones women suffer from. Poor men, they're as confused and vulnerable to the system and expectations that shape our lives as we are.

THE VULNERABLE MAN

I can want sex all I want, but the woman makes the decision.
She has the ultimate power over sex.

Lewis, 36

Let's talk about power, sexual power, I often do in my seminars. We debate who has it, and the first unthinking answer
is "Men." They still, for the most part, do the selecting, the
initiating dance in the sexual rites. Even today relatively few
women ask men for the first date, or suggest they engage in
sexual activity, much less "pop the question."

But, in a negative sense, we determine the outcome of all
those activities. We decide whether or not to spend the evening with a particular man, if we'll dance, if the evening will
end with sex. A man may ask, but a woman controls through
her answer. So a woman not only has the real power, she
wields it over a man when he is most vulnerable, in having
given in to his need for her. A woman's refusal can deny a
man fulfillment. If sexual intercourse repeats the acquisition
of manliness for a male, rejection leaves him powerless, child-
like, susceptible to the object of his desire. The power of rejection is particularly damaging because it depends on his
vulnerability alone.

The traditional supply-and-demand nature of sexual bargaining takes direct aim at men's vulnerability. Sex as a commodity creates the situation of women trying to conserve their
resources and men trying to convince women to grant them
sex. As long as a man must initiate this bargaining, he's in a
risk-taking position. Nancy Friday found that "women have
always derived power from the withholding of sex, which
means that throughout their lives, men experience women
negatively, as nay-sayers. From infancy, it's a female, the
mother, who has control over the way the male child experiences his body; we are the ones who lay down the rules and

conditions. A man doesn't say to a woman 'you cannot touch me until you do this; you can't do anything until you promise to love me forever.' Now this power in women produces an enormous rage in men but since their need for us is equally powerful, they bury their anger. It might be a happier world if women could just offer their bodies as men do, gladly and without condition."[1]

A man has a hard time understanding *why* a woman would refuse what seems to him a fundamentally pleasant experience. "My credo is all sex is good and some is better. Under that circumstance, withholding sex is simply a missed opportunity," was how one fifty-seven-year-old civil servant put it.

Tom, a twenty-four-year-old business machine salesman, echoed Nancy Friday when he said to me, "I can't understand why women feel they don't want to have sex, and why it wouldn't seem an enjoyable way to spend time. If we could all just get into it for the pure hell of it, we'd have a lot better time. Who knows, maybe one of those great physical experiences could lead naturally to something more, given time and mutual inclination."

Women seem convinced that they have little power over sex unless they hoard it. The male as sexual aggressor continues to be the standard role, and he has the first move in the negotiations. But *first* does not equal power but, in reality, vulnerability. Joyce, a psychotherapist with a good sense of the nature of sexual power-brokering, put it this way: "I feel that women have more power; besides the power of refusal, they have the power of contraception, and their bodies are so marvelous that they are not susceptible to equipment failure like men's."

In an ironic reverse, a man may feel that he has earned points (and thus gained power—or at least consideration) because he has allowed a woman to call the shots. He didn't take advantage of his superior strength and force himself on her: he asked, and asking, according to Elizabeth Janeway, "comes to feel to him, not just a first step in the bargaining process but a favor already granted. He has not simply advanced the proposition that they go to bed together, he has paid part of the price for getting the answer 'yes' and he expects that his downpayment will carry some weight. After he asks enough times he feels that the answer 'yes' is really due him. A woman can say no a few times, but not for long."[2]

When a woman refuses to have sex , she must have a good reason: a simple "no" or "I don't feel like it" are no longer acceptable reasons. Men don't realize the pressure women feel, because they are so rarely put in the position of responding to a sexual demand. When a man doesn't want to have sex, he simply doesn't ask. He keeps the bargaining to a minimum to avoid potential—and painful—rejection. Ironically, a woman doesn't see this as a loss of power to grant or withhold sex because she is unaware that he isn't asking.

YES + NO = MAYBE

If the bodies of all of us overly verbal, ambivalent, guilt-ridden, urban, middle-class, young Jews had been wired for sound and plugged into a public address system, the streets of our cities and campuses would have reverberated with a thunderous chorus of JUST LET ME SLEEP ALL NIGHT WITH MY ARMS AROUND YOU AND I PROMISE I WON'T TOUCH YOU! and JUST LET ME TOUCH YOU THERE AND I PROMISE I WON'T GO ANY FURTHER UNLESS YOU WANT ME TO! and JUST LET ME PUT THE TIP IN AND I PROMISE I WON'T GO IN ALL THE WAY UNLESS YOU ASK ME TO! and JUST LET ME PUT IT IN ALL THE WAY AND I SWEAR TO YOU I WON'T COME UNLESS YOU BEG ME TO.

Dan Greenburg, Scoring[3]

This may sound like an outmoded, old-fashioned situation from the ancient history of pre–sexual revolution days. But most men who read this passage have a high recognition factor: they tell me it's far from unusual to find themselves in situations where women expect them to plead for sex.

I still find that I have to sweet-talk a woman into having sex, at least the first few times we're together. Women say they want sex, but I think they don't want to take responsibility for their own actions.

George, 35

Because we feel so conflicted over whether or not to say "yes," often our "no" sound like a "maybe." Like "convince me." Men accuse women of saying no simply as an exercise in power, a testing of wills. While we are reluctant to admit it, we do enjoy the sense of being greatly desired, of being special, that "convincing" implies. A Good Girl needs a certain amount of persuasion or stimulation to change the "no" to a "yes."

Even in long-term committed relationships we want to be wooed, persuaded. And we still use our power to say no or yes to keep our man in line. "Who," asks a women I spoke with, "wants to be taken for granted? I can't have sex just because my loving husband wants to. I have to feel he really desires me, and our relationship has to be on good terms. When I am angry with him I can't always relax and forget that I feel upset. Even when I feel turned on I often hold back because I don't want him to think sex can make everything okay without working it out. So what usually happens after a disagreement, when he wants to make up via sex, is that I put him off. But he continues to try to turn me on because he knows that I almost always get turned on and forget about being mad." Note that she "almost" always allows herself to enjoy having sex when she started out adamantly not going to have sex. but not "always" or "never."

Every woman I know has, at some time in her life, said no when she really wanted to say yes to to sex. The Nuance perfume television commercial dramatizes the mechanism. One beautiful woman after another looks into the mirror with a sexy pout, dabbing the perfume on as she softly utters "No." Until the final frame, the final flirtatious female. She eyes the camera coyly, gives a little giggle, and says "Maybe."

Sociologist Jessie Bernard recognizes the tactic. "Often the verbal message is a bow in the direction of conscience or the mores and conventions, and the body signs and signals carry the real message. This does not necessarily mean that she . . . is speaking with a 'forked tongue.' She believes her words."[4] And confuses her men.

It's a double bind for the man: if he responds to the verbal message, he doesn't get what *he* wants. If he responds to the unspoken "yes," the "Sweep me away," he lays himself open to rejection or accusations of trying to impose his will. A woman hedges her bets: she gets what she wants—sex—without exposing herself either to societal condemnation or personal rejection.

Janeway says, "The greater his need, the greater his anxiety, for at the very heart of desire lies the possibility of its denial. The woman can refuse him absolutely or, perhaps worse, can mingle acceptance with withdrawal by lack of response. She may give herself only grudgingly and stint him in half a hundred ways that leave him with an angry residue of humiliation or that at the very least exact gratitude: an emotion that can only be pure if it's spontaneous."[5]

We feel that we have to say yes to sex to keep our options open for furthering a relationship but have to say no to maintain our Good Girl status. The compromise comes out as "maybe," which is so ambivalent that the man—left naked and vulnerable by his desire—"builds up a deep fear of rejection or vulnerability; that in turn forms a defense mechanism whereby men turn women into sex objects. Men intuitively discover that it hurts less to be rejected by an object than by a full human being. . . . Some women wonder why men rush into sex. Presumably, they are saying they don't take the initiative because they don't want sex as early as men do. 'Why can't men let a friendship evolve first?' they ask. Because once sex is a possibility, then the longer the period of potential rejection for the man. In order to shorten the period of potential rejection, men must activate their sexuality," writes Warren Farrell.[6] The "maybe" response, taken too far, pushes and exposes the man too much for his own comfort. He may simply drop out of the contest, or he may topple the Good Girl from her pedestal: she becomes the witholding bitch, the tease.

SWEET SOMETHINGS

You would think saying "I love you" to a woman to thrill and entice her isn't necessary anymore. But that's not so. These three words have a toniclike effect. I blurt out a declaration of love whenever I'm in the heat of passion. I'm not always believed, but it adds to the occasion for both of us. It's not exactly a deception on my part, I have to feel *something* for her. And, what the hell, it usually seems like the right thing to say at the time.

Bill, 33

Attempting both to shorten the period of potential anxiety and to fulfill a woman's demand to be seduced is a tall order, and there is evidence that a great deal of deception is the result of the barter woman effect: "Talk me into sex, fill my ears with sweet talk or I will withhold sex from you." Dr. Robert Staples found that women, in some cases, objected not to the sexual relationship but to the means used in pursuing it. "A number of them commented on the tendency of men to be very direct in stating their sexual desire. Many women prefer more ritual or flirtation."[7]

The sweet nothings murmured into a woman's ear are really anything but nothing: "You're so sexy," "I love you," "You're the best," tell a woman that she, and therefore this experience, is special. Kinsey's studies showed that "women responded more to words than to many other kinds of sexual stimulation. . . . [I]f men could be persuaded, they would find that ten minutes of tender words, loving words, gentle words, appreciative words were worth twice the amount of time spent in silent pawing. Indeed, without the words, the pawing may not even excite women. Sweetheart, honey, darling, even a plain but heartfelt 'dear' can be the open sesame."[8]

The conventional wisdom that "a hard penis has no conscience," that it is a man's right to resort to lying to get sexual satisfaction, may in reality be a man's behavioral response to a woman's demand to sanction sex and remain a Good Girl by being Swept Away.

> I don't understand why a man would take so much trouble and expense—drinks, dancing, dinner, a movie—all for a roll in the hay. I'm not a sex bomb.
>
> *Pamela*

The answer may be that subconsciously it's what women demand: attention, verbal caressing. *And as long as a woman contributes to a man's sexual anxiety by placing the burden of their potential relationship solely on him and his success as a seducer, he will try to allay that anxiety as quickly as possible by attempting sexual consummation.* Our demand to be Swept Away feeds directly into the masculine behavior we find upsetting.

A FANTASY FOR ONE

Writer David Bradley points out the result of these sexual bargains. "What makes me angriest of all is the childish assumption at the basis of this whole passion play: that a woman somehow has a right to have her fantasies fulfilled, that because she decides it's time for a romantic voyage, the man she chooses has to sign aboard for the cruise . . . nor does she have the right to expect that, simply because she has chosen to behave in a certain way, he must respond, not only as she wishes, but at all. The fact that she does not have such rights has nothing to do with a Male Conspiracy, or with gender at all: it has to do with reality. Because none of us has such rights, and those who expect them should grow up."[9]

Harsh words, but a valuable lesson. If we dream a fantasy that's unfulfilled, it would be wise to check and make sure it's not just a fantasy for one. We may sputter and fume and blame and complain, but the fault's our own.

SONS AND MOTHERS

Women exert power over men from the cradle on. We are the mirrors of generations of women behind us, reflecting and refracting mores and customs, and it would seem natural that men would see their paternity stretching backward in the distant perspective of their sexual glass. But despite the new fashionableness of shared parenting, most men and women today were raised by women. The father, until very recently, has been for the most part an absentee parent; provider, but not nurturer. The mother has been the child-rearer and character-molder. Our early education is still at the hands of women, from day-care attendants to elementary school teachers to Cub Scout den mothers. Men today have grown up mostly in a world of women. They tend to consult their mothers—or at least follow what they perceive as their example— rather than their fathers when it comes to doing the right thing about sex: not technique, but the rules of the game. They may get some details and encouragement from father–son talk, but selecting what kind of woman is right for them is usually a mother–son understanding.

The same rules and pressures, the same social and personal standards, that taught us to be Good Girls influence what our sons and brothers have learned: some women are virtuous, worhty of respect; some woman are Bad Girls.. But where do you draw the line?

A male child's sexual conditioning teaches him to compartmentalize his feelings for women into two categories: sexual and nonsexual. A developing boy cannot ignore his arousal: his penis points the way, and it is an independent organ, unfettered by society's incest taboos or the fine line that divides women into "touchable" or "untouchable." A sister, a neighbor, even a woman on a bus or a photograph of a complete stranger—all can trigger a young boy's sexual response. Willpower, socialization, and maturing physical control are necessary before the response can be limited to socially approved females. This sorting out is a big task, more than a young boy's unconscious mind—already at odds with his rebellious and independent organ—can handle. While young girls learn to divert and disguise their sexual feelings, young boys learn to divide them between nonsexual (mother, sister, teacher, authority figures) and sexual (all other women).

The division—woman as goddess or devil, as virgin or whore—is socially controlled by the same type of norms that enforce the stereotype of the Good Girl, and one of the most powerful lessons a boy learns is that these values are taught not only by older and wiser men, but by *women* themselves.

There's a great deal of anxiety inherent in this division, especially when it's overlaid with the lesson of the Good Girl— a being, like mother, not sexual in her own right, but one whom a boy must *make sexual.* He wants sex with a social equal, but he must do what he's been taught *not* to—arouse her, seduce her, break a taboo—to get what he wants.

Susan Locke, an associate professor of psychology at New York City's Baruch College, described an extreme result of this compartmentalization. One of her patients lived with a man for three years; their sex life was regular and active. Then they decided to get married and "he became totally asexual . . . he could have a sexual roommate, but not a sexual wife. His image of what a wife should be was almost antithetical to sex —a mother figure, a good girl, as opposed to the bad girl you sleep with." [10]

When a woman breaches the expectations a man has of her

sexuality, when she declines to be subject to the sexual compartmentalization he's been taught, it's equally confusing and
painful, as Myra, a twenty-seven-year-old administrative assistant, found out. "I met a guy at a singles dance place and
there was immediate attraction. After fending him off for the
first two times *I* decided to sleep with him the third time. My
taking the initiative freaked him out and I knew the next morning that he wouldn't call me. He wanted to make a conquest
and I had denied him that." She was bitter, but I'm sure he
was not pleased by the outcome of their evening, either. But
if you've learned that Good Girls must *be seduced*, it stands to
reason that the woman who *seduces* is bad.

If a man succeeds in negotiating the tricky shoals of who is
seducible and who isn't, and if his own sexuality isn't imper-
iled in the transaction, he still has to contend with the old code
that says that he's responsible for her for the rest of her life.
Now we know this is no longer true, but in the same way that
women have lingering attacks of Good Girl's guilt and Good
Girl's anxiety, a man may still be burdened with archaic notions of being roped and saddled, tied down, branded for life,
and all those other old-fashioned cowboy metaphors for an
entrapping relationship.

THE NEW MALE

I'm forty years old and for twenty years I've been trying to figure
out a satisfying, equal way to have a relationship. I cook, I clean,
I sew, I split household responsibilities. I sound to myself like
an ad for the perfect domestic creature. But I know that I have
regressions, flare-ups. I'm *not* free of old stereotypes I learned
watching my parents. But I know it, and I'm trying.

Jason, 40

The sexual revolution may feel to women like it's a man's
triumph, but to men it is a Pyrrhic victory. Marketing adviser

Daniel Yankelovich sees "an enormous increase in confusion among men, especially young men, as they search for a male role substitute for exclusive provider."[11] And Dr. Beverly Hotchner says, "One of the biggest problems I see in my office today is men beginning to panic. They say it just isn't there—whatever *it* is—for them in life. They are experiencing shrinking options."

The male vanguard of the late 1980s appears to be midway between old and new definitions: there's an exploration into rights and responsibilities, a search for a balance between personal options and economic security. Can men risk letting go of having to make it to the top of their careers, and if so, can they count on the psychological security of being accepted by women, and by their peers? And if careerism isn't the answer to self-fulfillment, what is? What will replace the struggle for the top and make life worth living? Is it personal relationships?

Most men, like most women, are bewildered and ambivalent about the role of sex and love in their lives and the lives of the women they know. On the one hand, they can't understand the residual resistance they're encountering, despite the sexual revolution. "I don't get it. Why is there still so much guilt about having sex? It seems to me that women still want to put on the brakes instead of letting themselves go. What was the sense of all the changes of the sixties, of the 'new morality,' if women don't allow themselves to be free to enjoy it?" asked an anonymous respondent.

Julian, twenty-four, voiced a common complaint I heard from men. "Women pretend to be so liberated but they don't act any different from the women in the fifties who wanted marriage as a payoff for having sex. Only now we call it a relationship."

On a short flight from New York to Vermont, I got into a conversation with my seatmate, Emerson. He appeared to be in his mid-forties, was handsome, slightly graying, an executive in television. I gathered material wherever I could find it, so I grilled him about men and women and sex and love, 1980s style.

"There's a common scenario that I go through," he told me. "I meet a woman, and in the world I'm in, she's usually a supercharged career woman anxious to let me know right away that she can't be distracted from her goals. She's only interested in the present, in a dinner now and then, some companionship, occasional sex. And I think, 'Terrific, a meeting of minds.'

"We're just beginning to know each other, to find out if we have anything in common, when BANG, the 'relationship' talk!

"It's inevitably after the third time we've slept together. She sits me down. 'Where is this all going?' she asks. 'What's this relationship to you?' The next step is that she tries to get me to declare love for her and make a commitment. What happened to the original deal, I always wonder. And then *I* walk away from the so-called 'relationship.' "

We think men are speedy about sexual relationships. But men are often stunned by the rapidity with which a self-proclaimed liberated woman reverts to a love-needy and dependent type who insists the deal is still sex for security.

We've really bottomed out on instant sex. In the sixties and seventies we were designing comments: "We came together! We fused chemically! We lit up the sky!" That was romantic thinking. But that all sounds like a lot of motel art to me now. I know people who got that sexual experimentation, out-for-me-only, can't-settle-down bone in their teeth in the sixties and seventies and they can't let go even now. I see them as frighteningly solitary people and I'm sad for them. . . . The freedom we have now gives us the ability to appreciate the genuinely, deeply attractive things in the opposite sex, not just flashy externals. Now that the novelty of license has worn off, we can get down to what's really important.

Tom McGuane[12]

Men *are* changing. It may have happened to them at a different time in history than to us, but there is a sense, especially among younger men, that the old values of the macho, corporate male were neither life-enhancing nor, in the final analysis, pleasurable. Dr. Michael Carrera says, "I don't subscribe to the notion that women have a greater emotional investment in sex, whereas men are more interested in physical release. That's a stereotype which should be undone in the '80's, just as women's lib undid so many old myths in the '70's. Certain men, like certain women, are extremely emotional about sex." [13]

> I had hoped that something long-lasting and emotionally deep would develop from our sleeping together. Unfortunately, we had known each other for a very short while and it turned out we were too different. I felt much guilt and disappointment.
>
> *Nash, 21*

Nash is a new male; his values are much more likely to coincide with women's—the desire for commitment, caring, the sense of "shrinking options" when a relationship fails. While women are learning to undo the myths of the Good Girl, disencumbering themselves of the old assumptions and conventions, men too are beginning to break the old patterns and to struggle to create new, positive ones. If we look around, we can meet some of these new males:

> I've found the type of man I can love; he's relieved to relinquish responsibility and therefore the power that the old sex roles compelled him to take.
>
> *Sheila*

But we—men and women—send such mixed signals about what we want and what we need. Publisher Michael Korda speaks of the confusion men are feeling: "All of their experience teaches them that while women claim to like sensitive men, in fact they often prefer aggressive, powerful, macho take-charge guys . . . the high school football star makes out better, as a rule, than the school's top scholar. What's more (and maybe more important), masculine society—the male peer group—generally values toughness above sensitivity, physical strength and athletic ability above intellectual achievement, action above feeling."[14] Men risk as much as women in their struggle to achieve a new way of being and relating.

And we still demand more; admit it, we want an understanding he-man, a man Korda labels "the sensitive brute." We want a man who combines traditional masculinity with the ability to communicate and be intimate. We want a lover who's sexy and impulsive and at the same time caring and protective. We're demanding the old—economic support—and the new —emotional support. Put this way, doesn't that seem like a lot of demanding for one poor human soul to live up to, male or female? Until we can take responsibility as well as give it away, this muddle will remain.

10

INVENTING YOURSELF

DISCARDING STEREOTYPES

I've learned in the last few years that I'm a whole and valuable person instead of an adjunct to a man or a family. As I grow more sure of myself, what I want and what I can give, I have options that I didn't realize existed before. I like that.

Elizabeth, 55

I like this woman so much, her optimism and self-value. This chapter was the most fun to write because it's filled with examples and advice from women who are strong, together, positive. We know we can't be perfect all the time, that our decisions won't always be the right ones, that we will be susceptible to hurt and disappointment—it's part of life. But to judge from the women who sent me their recipes for getting on with it, for living and loving with maximum pleasure, we're really cooking.

To understand why we get Swept Away is to understand our personal contradictions and those in the world spinning around us. In the pages ahead, men and women who have thought all this over and have come away with some ideas offer their experiences, perspectives, and support to help clarify options for changing.

Invent yourself. That's my advice. Learn from everyone around you; know that nothing is static, nothing sacred about sex and love except what makes you feel good and right. Know, too, that simply recognizing the forces at work around you—and *on* you—will give you strength and understanding to make things the way *you* want them.

> We have seen stereotypes come and go in our time—from the "virtuous" non-sexual woman to the lusty, genitally-oriented women of the Masters and Johnson era, to the spiritualized, sisterly lover of the late seventies. If we enter the eighties with no clear, sharp-edged notion of what our sexuality is or "should be"—and with no consensus on the role of sex in our lives (and in our revolution)—this should not be dismaying.
>
> *Rayna Rapp*[1]

As Alex Comfort writes, "This is the first generation that Western society has called upon to make a truly moral, intelligent choice of sexual life-styles. Other generations were spared the choice by virtue of social strait-jackets imposed on them."[2] Let's take advantage of this. We have the best chance in history to achieve a balance of sexual satisfaction and intimacy in our lives without the excess baggage of guilt, fear, and uncertainty that has sabotaged women's sexual joy in the past. Things aren't perfect yet, but we can't stop trying.

Inevitably there will be tension and ambivalence in women's progress. If we want to affirm our sexuality and our right to develop as sexual beings, we *will* run into resistance from men, other women, from ourselves. Even our rights to use contraception will continue to be challenged. "I think we tend to feel the battle is won, when the struggle to use birth control to free women for honest choices about their own sexuality hasn't even begun," writes Jill Conway, president of Smith College. And she adds, "Women are not accepted yet as fully sexual beings who have their own choices and their own needs. If we think there are any profession[s] in this country

[that] really accept a self-defining female, or a majority of whose members accept that, we are seriously misleading one another."[3] But if we don't try, we narrow our boundaries and sublimate our energy; our options and maturity are curtailed.

And if we don't try, we will perpetuate the same old repressive patterns and sexual confusions in the women who follow us—our younger sisters, our daughters, our friends. We can make a tremendous difference in other women's lives by taking that first determined step for ourselves.

SEX MATTERS

Sex is not a three-letter word for love. Sex is a physical act, physiological response to sexual stimuli. Sex charges the atmosphere and complicates communication between a man and a woman. Sex can create a deeper bond between two people, enriching what is already a bonding relationship. Or it can put a damper on a relationship that might have developed into a lasting friendship. But no matter, we have to stop downgrading it, saying it isn't really important to us.

It is easier to admit to a hungering for romance. Yet a recent study found that conceptions of romance were contradictory. Most men and women agreed that "walks on a moonlit beach, declarations of love, and kisses in public are romantic. But when asked to describe an especially romantic episode, one in five tells of an unusual or exciting sexual adventure."[4]

Joyce, a woman in her late thirties, has taken a realistic look at where she places sex: "I have to admit that all of the serious relationships I have had were with men with whom I enjoyed having sex. If a man and I aren't sexually compatible, I know the relationship won't last. I love having sex too much." Too cold-hearted? Are you saying, "What about loving feelings, caring for each other: doesn't that count for something?" Of course, but so does sexual attraction and compatibility. Placing a good sexual relationship on your list of priorities doesn't eliminate the importance of affection and deep feelings for a man. It's merely realistic. Like Joyce, women need to accept their sensual feelings, declare they are erotic, physical. We can reap the benefits of the changes in our cultural ideas about sexual behavior by letting ourselves be first and foremost in charge of our own sexuality.

WHAT ARE YOU DOING FOR THE REST OF YOUR LIFE?

Loving is such a wonderful way to feel—to give *and* receive. If there is hurt, it goes away. And we all end up richer for sharing our lives. Sharing, learning to be open to others, can only expand our own horizons.

Joan, 36

There's a new frontier out there, one that needs exploring and taming. It's the Wild West of true sexual equality, the equality that comes from women taking responsibility for at least half of the sexual experience. Waiting for someone else to thrill us romantically doesn't get the job done.

Part of our fear is tied up with rejection: what if he isn't interested? We learned that rejection is a life-or-death matter instead of the other side of the coin of acceptance. Having women take their place alongside men and be governed by the same sexual rules is such a truly new idea that it is bound to cause heart palpitations because, as Warren Farrell points out, "We have been misled by the fact that sex is more available. What has remained the same is the expectation that the man will do the initiating and risk rejection at every stage of sexual interest, whether first hand-holding or first touching of tongues. . . . Sharing the sexual initiative would enhance women's ability to take professional and personal risks and spare men becoming prisoners of success and power as a way of attracting women without being rejected. For both our sakes, sharing the sexual initiative is the next giant step for women and men to take together."[5]

It may even be that a woman would be better off approaching men who appeal to her rather than waiting for men to whom she appeals. It's more likely that the man who "comes on strong," who is still invested in the old ways of men and women, will be the one she meets, while the sensitive, introverted man looking for a new kind of relationship is waiting for *her* to make the first move.

> CHEERFUL, CLAUSTROPHOBIC, goodlooking bad bet, wants to be swept off her feet, or have them placed on firm ground, or something, by divinely attractive, moderately difficult, highly intelligent man around forty, or fifty, divorced at least once would be good. Divinely is asking too much, but what the hell, it's my nickel. . . .[6]

I had to applaud the woman who placed this ad; she was setting out to find romance on her terms, and a man to *her* liking. I admire her spunk. "When a woman takes control, or at least shares it, she becomes the buyer," advises Natalie Mackler. "Sex is initiated because of mutual interest, not because of relinquishing autonomy. This boosts confidence when you are the chooser as well as the chosen. The relationship has a more stable and equal beginning, and as a side benefit, a woman's pool of eligible men expands. Love is something we have been told to aspire to all of our lives. Mapping a more self-interested path is going to take a woman a while."

> Take control of your life. Make decisions about your life and arrange to make those things happen. If you respect yourself, your decisions and priorities, I find that it generally follows that you don't need another person—you have yourself. And then it seems that it's easier to find and enjoy someone and for that person to enjoy you.
>
> *Sheila*

As we get more hardy, we will learn to be less ambivalent and more able to make our own decisions based on what we want, not what someone else has told us is good for us.

HONORABLE INTENTIONS

I don't think we ought to live without romance. But I think we need to be realistic about adapting our romantic notions to fit our new lives. Our old fantasy required red roses, candlelight dinners quietly served in an elegant atmosphere, long leisurely kisses. Maybe we need to see daisies in a bunch bought at the subway, fried chicken from a box, and making love on Sunday morning before the noise of the neighborhood gets annoying, as real romance.

Janet, 33

The most difficult thing I find about close relationships is getting close and staying equal. There are always difficulties when two "whole" people merge toward intimacy.

Anonymous, 55

"At what point is it fair to expect commitment?" was the question posed by Joanne, a woman in my seminar, who to my surprise was married. It took me aback. But the tension between men and women over the meaning of commitment can be found in any type of relationship. Commitment isn't sharing the same abode, the same bed, or having a legal document binding you together; it is an emotional declaration that is backed up with considerate, loyal, and supportive behavior.

Fathers used to ask men if their intentions were honorable. This routine, of course, had the advantage of weeding out men with honorable intentions from those we can presume just wanted to fool around. The inquiry into intentions has been replaced by investigating a man's commitment, but now women do it. The problem here is that there is never a point when you can ask a man *for* commitment; it isn't something you can request. Like love, like loyalty, commitment comes from within. It can't be forced; it isn't an obligation. It develops over sharing experiences, tolerance, building trust, and the special sense of having a unique caring relationship. The only aspect of commitment you can control is your *own* feelings and intentions.

In a relationship you can declare that you are committed, and then lay out what this commitment means to you: sharing his life, building a nest, having children, hiking together, spending *all* weekend together, or however you define it. But you have to spell it out. Commitment is a chameleon; it has any number of meanings and nuances. To some it means forever, for better or worse; for others commitment is for the here and now and is renegotiable at every point. It is fair, and prudent, to ask a man what is his commitment to you, to clarify his intentions involving his future with you. But not until you have sorted out the depth and width of *your* own commitment first.

First, we must deal with why we feel compelled to want commitment from this specific man. Is it commitment we want from any man, and is this one the most likely candidate? We have to check out our vulnerability level and decide if we are acting out of some version of the veiled contract rather than a mutual and genuine relationship. And a woman has to be realistic about the physiological processes that are affecting her. Is it the ticking of the biological clock? For women in their late thirties, edging toward the possibility of never being a mother, it may be the fear that they won't find a man to father a child and share childrearing with. While some women go it alone without commitment from a man, most of us want a man to share the joys and the burdens of parenting.

Or is it that we see ourselves changing when we look into the mirror? There is still the fear—no, let's face it, the terror—of aging. A woman past forty no longer is relegated to the old folks' home, but we aren't naïve enough to assume that a woman's age doesn't matter. That hasn't happened yet. While we are seeing some younger men with older women, men predictably are attracted to a woman younger than they are. So women can feel they are facing decreasing opportunities with no time to lose. But women feel the pressure of being told they are pushing too hard, too soon by men who don't have the same need to move on with it. Men don't have to deal with biological limitations or becoming a cast-off in middle age. They can father children as senior citizens, and date or mate with women half, or even a quarter, their age.

But women should examine their timing, whether they *are* forcing the issue. We would never expect loyalty and devotion from a woman friend based on a few dinners, a show or two, days or even weeks of sharing sun and sand on a Mexican beach. We try to be picky, choosy about our friends. We know that a committed friendship takes time, energy, trust, is sometimes inconvenient, and that we are expected to be there in foul weather, remember birthdays, and split the cost of doing things together. Sharing bed and board with a man has to be at least as serious and twice as complicated as developing a female friendship.

MR. RIGHT REDUX

We need to look critically at the men in our lives and our ways of picking and choosing. We're impractical about choosing a man who will help us "merge toward intimacy"; our expectations are informed by old myths. *We must learn to put our energy where it makes sense, to reach out for commitment from men who have characteristics that we really want, not characteristics that we've created.* "The problem is that women are not seeking a man who will fit into the kind of life they want for *themselves*," says Natalie Mackler. "For example, a client of mine, who was twenty-six years old, was feeling worried because she didn't have a serious man in her life. I asked her if serious meant marriage. She said it did and pegged thirty-two as the best age to marry because she wanted children, at least one. I asked her why she was unhappy about the lack of a serious relationship, when she didn't really want one for at least six years. I suggested she enjoy meeting many different men, spend time doing what she wanted to do, and then put her efforts into a serious relationship when the timing was right for her."

We need to ask ourselves an important question: What kind of life do I want for myself? And the answer may not be the old forms: marriage, children, the slender gold band. Trying to force ourselves into that mold can be a trap, too. We have to look at what daily life with a prospective lover, a serious one, would be like. His life plans and life-style will have an impact on ours. Carpenters, jazz musicians, and corporate executives live very different lives. If he is a professional ball player, he will be on the road a lot. If he is an accountant, his hours will probably be regular, and he will be around to do things with. Do we want a life with a lot of free time, independence, or do we want to snuggle in, spend evenings, all of them, in the bliss of his company? Stars in our eyes only lead to Mr. Right blindness. Once we stop being vague about "happily-ever-after," we may realize that what we, and he, want out of life isn't compatible and a commitment would only make it worse.

And perhaps most important, we need to acknowledge that *there is no Mr. Right*—just another imperfect, struggling human being.

We can examine why a man might not only be hesitant about being committed, but deeply reluctant. Anthony Brandt, a writer, gives us some perceptive insight. He is blunt: "I think [men] are afraid. I sense in them not a fear of women but of a relationship in which they don't know who they are, what role they are expected to play, a relationship in which, because there are no fixed rules anymore, they will have to fight to retain some sense of themselves as men."[7] Paul, who is in his early twenties, talks about why he and a woman he "really cared about" broke up: "I couldn't live up to her expectations. She and I were both working on commission, but I was expected to earn more money than she did. And we talked about having kids. She expected me to be the breadwinner, and clean, and cook, and share child rearing, but I was supposed to be the one in charge of everything that needed fixing and make all the tough decisions. It was too much." Women's need to have a man be Mr. Right, a man without warts, puts men on the defensive. They feel exposed, vulnerable, their "usual ways of dealing with women, their idea of what makes a woman sexy and desirable, their sense of their power and authority in the family, their dedication to their careers, have all come under attack."[8]

Men know that Mr. Right is powerful, successful. That, of course, is the final irony of the situation. A lot of men want to retire the mantle of Mr. Right: being perfect, all-knowing, dominant. One man put it this way: "I'm just an ordinary guy wanting to be loved and love a woman in return." If a woman wants to share her life with a man, she can readjust the rose-colored glasses.

> It's been ages since I felt that giddiness of "falling in love." Infatuation makes my stomach queasy and sets up horrible fears in my mind that I could lose myself. I'm always reminding myself that this is only a man and soon enough some little habit one of us has will get on the other's nerves. At that point we will need to take a rational look and decide what's really going on in the relationship and if we have enough potential to work on something together.
>
> *Sheila*

Or, as a single twenty-nine-year-old woman who is inventing herself wrote, "Be realistic about love or you will miss a lot of the pleasures that reality can bring."

TORTOISE OR HARE?

We can never go back to the old ways; even if the pendulum of history swings backward, it doesn't make a full stroke. Neither will we stay in the furthest outposts of the new sexual frontiers; typically, the sexual revolution mimicked other political and behavioral revolutions through the centuries by going to extremes in order to bring about change. You may feel like a lumbering tortoise, left in the dust by a quick-running set of sexual rabbits, or like a hare ahead of the game, impatient with the lagging turtles.

The truth probably is that you're both, and the less you feel pushed to the extremes of either sexual freedom or sexual regression, the less you will need to fall back on any one particular stance. Karolyn, a divorced gallery director of thirty-seven, cautions, "Don't have sex or fall in love because you feel it is the obvious thing to do. Do not confuse the terms or expect always to find them together."

A recent survey indicates that women are beginning to seek the level of sexual activity that is most comfortable to them. Half the single women went to bed with a man on the first or second date, for instance. But if 50 percent of these women were having sex at that point, the other 50 percent weren't— an even split.[9] *There is no one sexual revolution;* we must learn to follow our feelings, invent ourselves, and act on whatever we feel is best for us.

> I find that I do much better if I just tell a man directly on the first date that I fall in "puppy love" when I have sex and that I can't stand the trauma of first-date sex. If he gets skittish, or pressures me, then there usually is no second date. But at least I don't have to keep patching up a wounded ego and a cracked heart because he didn't call. I've also discovered that most men I've leveled with seem to understand and don't pressure me. In fact, I think it has made a tremendous difference in how I am devel-

oping relationships with men. And in a funny kind of way, waiting adds to the delights of sex. So I lose a few; better than kidding myself about a relationship.

Ann, 35

SLOWING DOWN IN THE EIGHTIES

Love can be a beautiful, satisfying experience if it is with the right person. Sex, too, can be very satisfying. Look inside yourself and discover what you like and live by that. Be careful and open-minded with your sexuality; don't use it to achieve instant intimacy, and don't try to substitute sex for love.

Anonymous, 29

Take time out to catch your breath and generally stand back to examine the need to find love in every sexual relationship. Nancy Friday says, "Postponing sex until a friendship develops means we can deal more coolly with our expectations about the relationship. Sex has a way of re-arousing old— sometimes childish—expectations and fantasies about *what this man can do and be for us*. Knowing him first as a friend, as a totally separate person, with his own needs, problems, expectations and flaws, helps us maintain a degree of rational judgment when reality inevitably enters after the 'honeymoon.' The fall from high and romantic love—the illusion of love— will not be such a precipitous drop if the friendship was there first." [10]

Barbara Seaman wrote, "The backlash is against casual sex because a lot of people were hurt. It was as if there was a train gradually carrying us away from Victorian morality, but then suddenly in the sixties and seventies the train became a runaway, and a lot of passengers were injured. Now the brakes are starting to be repaired." [11] As our own self-value increases, so too does our selectivity toward both experience and partner.

"After my divorce seven years ago, I was so thrilled to be out in the singles world that I wasn't very selective about men. I was twenty-five; meeting men was easy." Jennifer, now in her early thirties, and I were watching the sun go down over a lake in upstate New York. We were both attending a conference at the Institute for Family Research and Education.

"As I got older, I got pickier," she continued. "Sometimes now I even feel panic about being able to find a satisfying relationship with one man. But most of the time, I'm content. It doesn't bother me if I don't have a date, as long as I have something to do with friends that I enjoy.

"But I'm still incredibly vulnerable at times: the end of a relationship I had for seven months last year was the turning point for me. I was ready to move forward—not into marriage, necessarily, but toward a more permanent commitment. We had a showdown, he left, and left me feeling amazed and hurt that I could have felt so much and he so little.

"I did a lot of soul-searching then. I actually sat down with a pencil and paper to analyze what had happened, because I knew I couldn't continue the date-around, get-close, break-up routine. I discovered that I was almost always in love with a man who didn't share the same *wow* feeling. It was an eye-opener.

"Once I owned up to liking to be in love, in one form or another, things began to fall into place. I had thought of myself as selective, and felt that my discrimination meant that my instant lovelike feelings resulted from the excellence of my choice in men. But in reality, my tendency to get too gushy and fall in love too fast means men are either put off—and they leave—or they take advantage of me—and they leave. They enjoy the sex but shrug off the love, leaving me hurt and miserable.

"So I made myself some 'calm down' rules. Whenever I feel turned on by a man I've just met, I take a mental count of ten and try to find a quiet place to think about what I'll do next;

I've done a lot of valuable thinking in the bathrooms of bars and restaurants. I have three categories of desire. First, am I looking mainly for a physical, sexual release? Would it be easier and less involved if I reached orgasm with my vibrator? Second, is intimacy my goal? Do I need to be hugged, cuddled, cared for? Would it be better not to get involved or to head for the hugs, come what may? And third, am I falling for the rush of romance, falling in love to fall in love? Is the fantasy better and more powerful than the reality will be?

"Sorting out those needs helps me to be clear about what's going on. And my final criterion is simple: would a sexual encounter with this man be good for me? If the answer is yes, if the event coincides with my own ethical code, if the result will be more self-satisfaction rather than less, well, then it's a go!

"I still get carried away by the emotion of the moment; the thrill of unexpected sex is wonderful. But because I've learned to identify the experience for what it is, I'm not devastated if I never see the guy again."

Slowing down in the eighties doesn't mean that we're wistful for the old forms and expectations. We know what Adrienne Rich said: "Nostalgia is only amnesia turned around." Some women are putting sex on hold because they feel they've had more sex than they want with men they didn't care about. Women make temporary decisions not to pursue sex because they are feeling disappointment, or seeking new ways to define their needs and power. We no longer "save ourselves" with the optimistic view that we will live happily ever after with the man of our dreams; we save ourselves because we know we're valuable.

When I feel I have to have a man in my life it diverts a lot of my energy. I can go for long periods of time without sex. I find that it clears my head; I free myself to see my friends, to have a new, refreshing look at life. It's only temporary, because I do enjoy sex. Some men see this as a challenge. I've learned to be direct and just say, "I hope we can continue being friends; right now I'm not interested in a sexual relationship."

Dorothy, mid-20s

IDENTIFYING EXPERIENCES

A short-term, fun-filled fling can be very helpful to a woman. It frees her to concentrate on physical pleasure because she's not emotionally entangled. It can be wonderful, thrilling; she can really experiment.

Beth Anne, graduate student

No-strings sex, sex that is not repeated or doesn't lead to long-term commitment, still has a place in our lives if we want it to. It can be a process, a way of getting to know a man, an opportunity rather than a form of second-rate experience. It can help a woman find out what the other person is like in an intimate way, and what she needs from a man. It can be constructive and successful if we don't misidentify it.

A brief erotic experience can also be a form of self-revelation. The anonymity frees us from responsibility; we can let ourselves go, revel in our own pleasure. With neither past nor future, there are no expectations about our own behavior, or his; no emotional entanglements to interfere with physical pleasure. One woman told me of the surprise she felt after her first "no strings" sexual experience. "I didn't pretend he was my one and only. He was simply my special someone for the moment. I found I could experience an emotion I had never really thought I was capable of—*lust!*"

Carol Callahan writes of learning to experiment with sex after her divorce. "Not that I became promiscuous, but I became quite adventurous—not so scared. . . . I needed to learn about myself, my own body, and different kinds of men. Not that it was easy; in fact, it was hard. Since I had not been raised with the new casual attitude toward sex, and since I had grown up thinking that sex and marriage were tied together, it took me quite a while before I could say 'yes' to a new man. But as I gradually became more confident of my own attractiveness to men, I began to change, and I actually *looked forward* to making love. I enjoyed the variety—I enjoyed dating and bedding this one and that one—and wondered how I could ever be faithful to one man again." [12]

Learning to identify various aspects of experience helps us invent ourselves. Sheri Tepper suggests different categories of sex to be aware of: "One is sex between acquaintances; that is, sex between people who, frankly, don't know each other very well. The sexual experience may be pleasantly repeated or you may never see one another again. Then there is sex between friends. Acquaintances do not owe each other anything but a courteous relationship, but friends begin to obligate themselves in a mutual understanding, an implied commitment. With an acquaintance you can say 'no, thank you' about sex and leave it at that. With a friend, you are expected to provide an explanation. Friendship implies that each person is committed to meeting at least some of the needs of the other person, whether it is convenient or not. The needs may or may not include sex. . . . If one is not certain of friendship, then one may decide to have a sexual relationship, but don't force something else out of it. Don't pursue, whine, demand, cry, throw tantrums, *or get pregnant*. Accept sex for what it is, for what pleasure it gives you. But don't demand that it mean any more to him than the pleasure it gives him. . . . Don't lie to yourself. Don't say, 'He really loves me, he just doesn't show it.' " [13]

SAFE SEX, NOT NO SEX

In today's world the existence of AIDS makes using good judgment about sex imperative. While abstaining from sex or being sure you are in a mutually monogamous relationship with someone who is free of the AIDS virus are the only sure fire guarantees that you won't be exposed, other choices about sexual relationships are still attainable—with responsibility. As the authors of *Safe Encounters* put it, "The AIDS epidemic has made it a matter of life and death that we change the old sexual expectation and habit of unprotected intercourse. To keep ourselves safe, we must develop new habits with each of our partners except those who can prove beyond a shadow of a doubt that they are HIV-negative." [13]

In practical terms, women must learn to protect themselves, by learning the facts about AIDS and by protecting safer sex techniques. It's a harsh reality, but *sex can have negative health consequences*. In general, the guidelines for safer sex are: limit the numbers of sex partners you have, choose your partners carefully, and use a latex condom each and every time you have sex. Obviously, you need more specifics about the transmission of AIDS and the details of safe sex and safer sex encounters. One good place for current information is the Public Health agency in your community.

At the core of Callahan and Tepper's messages is this: you can gain something from a sexual experience outside of a potential long-term monogamous relationship. There are many perfectly safe ways to express sexuality without giving up sensual pleasure and sexually intimate relationships. Just avoid spur-of-the-moment, damn the torpedoes, risky sexual behavior.

NO MORE TAKING CHANCES

Margaret Sanger, that feisty and courageous woman who went to jail to help women achieve the right to contraception, is one of my heroines. "No woman can call herself free . . . until she can choose whether or not to be a mother," she said, and I wholeheartedly agree.

Margaret Sanger won her battle: all women in this country

today have the right under law to access to birth control. It's up to us to seize this right, to use if *for ourselves*, to take responsibility for our contraceptive needs squarely and with forethought. We must admit, and learn to love, our sexuality; then we must learn to control the *results* of our sexuality.

We can avoid the fear, the emotional terror and economic havoc of unwanted pregnancy, by being realistic with ourselves. In the most practical sense, a woman must choose a method of birth control that fits her own personality and lifestyle. No contraception will work unless it is used properly, and this requires effort and concentration. It may even change the way a woman handles her sex life, but the change can only be for the better.

There are some thoughtful questions to consider in the process of making the choice of birth control. How good is your memory? Daily pill-taking must be rigorously on schedule to be effective. How much help can you expect from your partner, or how much participation do you want? Condoms, foam, and the rhythm method and natural family planning demand a high level of communication between partners about contraception, so use these methods only if you feel comfortable about discussing them. How do you feel about touching yourself? It's a necessary part of using foam, a diaphragm, a sponge, an IUD. How important is the illusion of spontaneity? You may need to use the Pill or an IUD to maintain the illusion. How often do you have sex? If frequently, using the diaphragm, sponge, foam, or a condom may be irritating; if infrequently, taking the Pill every day may seem remote. How would you feel if you became pregnant right now? The higher the risk, the more certain you'd better be of total protection.

The freedom of contraceptive choice means learning about *all* of the choices, and *using whichever method you choose consistently and effectively.*

THE BEST OF TIMES

For all of the shortcomings of the sexual revolution, for all of the turmoil that we've seen in our lives in the last twenty years, we are fortunate to live in this time and place. Our strengths are still ours—women's capacity to love and care for other people, our sense that there is more to the world than just the tangible. And our weaknesses too—but there is a rising tide of self-assurance that is the greatest antidote to the vulnerability and ambivalence we inherited.

Researcher Elizabeth Nickles is also optimistic about women gaining in self-confidence and independence. She identifies women she calls "pacesetters." Women who are energetic, educated, ambitious: women who write their own tickets. This group makes up 43 percent of all women and 57 percent of working women. "These women are unlike any large psychographic female group to date, not only in their characteristics, but equally important, in their widespread social acceptability and high status, which will allow them to grow and expand as a group, rather than be snuffed out by society as minority and so-called extremist groups have been in the past." [14]

> It is better to have been swept away than to suffer the ravages of self-inflicted guilt, but we have to stop hurting ourselves because we feel we have to adhere to a code we don't believe in anymore.
>
> *Anonymous*

Once we break the chains of our need to win the approval of others before we act sexually, our need to be Swept Away will wither away.

Once we learn to accept the reality that we can't please everyone all of the time, we can learn to please ourselves. The rest will follow.

Once we know what our culture, our religion, our parents,

and our lovers demand of us and why, we can let it go and make the changes in our own lives that work for us.

Once we accept that sex is not only a powerful force but a positive one, we will learn to be fully, responsibly sexual. A fully sexual woman is strong, independent, whole. And the paradox of a successful relationship is that two halves don't make a whole; two wholes do.

NO MORE FIREWORKS?

Does the thought of a life devoid of the thrill of passion and romance seem like heavy weather? Do you understand your need to be Swept Away in its social, historical, behavioral perspectives, and feel adult and in control? And yet does a small voice mutter in the back of your mind, "In too much control"?

Part of inventing yourself is permitting yourself the excitement of being suffused with love, burning with desire, without being consumed by the flames. One respondent sent in a poem a friend had written that expresses perfectly the ambivalent need even the most aware woman sometimes feels:

> Contentment is secure
> But the lure of touching ecstasy
> Makes me reach out again and again
> For otherwise how will I know
> When I'm holding it in my hand?[15]

"This means," she added, "we need to plant our feet firmly on the ground while reaching for the stars." You're permitted. It's allowed! *You allow yourself!* Hover around the candle; if you understand fire, you won't singe your wings. You'll enjoy the sparkle and glow of ecstasy and it will be better than ever.

NOTES

1: A COUNTERFEIT EMOTION

1. Barbara Cartland, *Dreams Do Come True* (New York: Bantam Books, 1981), p. 1.
2. From an advertising blurb on romance novels, Silhouette Book Club, 1981. The book cited is Mary Carroll's *Shadow and Sun*.
3. *Glamour*, September 1983, p. 198.
4. Among many important examples are: Pamela Lowry, "Unwanted Pregnancy—Why?" mimeographed paper from Planned Parenthood, 476 West MacArthur Blvd., Oakland, Calif. 94609. Published originally in *Harvard Crimson*, August 10, 1971; William B. Miller, "Psychological Vulnerability to Unwanted Pregnancy," *Family Planning Perspectives*, 5, 4 (1975), 199–201; also his chapter "The Psychological and Psychiatric Aspects of Population Problems" in D. A. Hamburg and H. K. Brodie, eds., *American Handbook of Psychiatry*, Vol. 4 (New York: Basic Books, 1973); Kristin Luker, *Taking Chances: Abortion and the Decision Not to Contracept* (Berkeley, Calif.: University of California Press, 1975); E. S. Herold and M. Goodin, "Measurement Issues Involved in Examining Contraceptive Use Among Young Single Women," unpublished paper, Department of Family Studies, University of Guelph, Ontario, Canada, 1980; Ira Reiss, *SIECUS* report, "Premarital Sexual Standards," Study Guide No. 5 (revised), 1975.
5. James McCary, *Human Sexuality*, 3rd ed. (New York: Van Nostrand, 1978), p. 283.
6. Greer Litton Fox, "Nice Girl: Social Control of Women Through Value Construct," *Signs*, 2 (1977), 805–817. See, specifically, foot-

note 33 where she lists a number of research sources that suggest the Swept Away phenomenon.

7. Lowry, "Unwanted Pregnancy—Why?"
8. Nancy Friday, *My Mother/My Self* (New York: Delacorte Press, 1977), p. 274 and p. 277.

2: THE VEILED CONTRACT

1. Poem from "A Morning Meditation," by Unknown, twelfth century, sent to me without citation.
2. There are many good resources, but a very good report is Martha Baum, "Love, Marriage and the Division of Labor," *Sociological Inquiry*, 41 (Winter 1978), 107–117. For a very helpful review of marriage as an exchange see Charles F. Westoff, "Some Speculations on the Future of Marriage and Fertility," in *Teenage Sexuality, Pregnancy and Childbearing* (New York: Alan Guttmacher Institute, 1981). For the influence of sociobiology on the exchange of sex and power see Irving Goffman, "The Arrangement Between the Sexes," in *Theory and Society* (Amsterdam: Elsevier Scientific Publishing Co., 1977).
3. Kenneth W. Eckhardt, "Exchange in Sexual Permissiveness," *Behavior Science Notes*, 1 (1971), 1–18.
4. An excellent article is Warren Farrell, "Risking Sexual Rejection: Women's Last Frontier?" *Ms.*, April 1982. The quote is on p. 100.
5. State statutes closely define the legality of the rites, although the specifics vary. But usually VD tests have to be passed and proof of age must be given. Only a state-approved magistrate, rabbi, minister, or priest can solemnize the ceremony, which includes a declaration by the parties of their intention to marry and vows of commitment. When the official representative of the state says, "By the power vested in me by the State of ———, I pronounce you husband and wife," the couple is declared legally married. The license must now be signed by the couple, witnesses, and the officiator and filed at the county courthouse.
6. See Landon Y. Jones, *Great Expectations and the Baby Boom Generation* (New York: Ballantine Books, 1980). Quote on p. 209.
7. From his column "If You Ask Me: It's Your Move, Men," *Washington Post*, August 3, 1983.
8. "Marital Status and Living Arrangements," *National Center for Health Statistics*, March 1982, and "Marrying, Divorcing, and Liv-

ing Together in the U.S. Today," *Population Bulletin,* 32, 5 (February 1979).
9. Quoted in "Cupid Slowing," *Albuquerque Tribune,* July 1, 1983.
10. Ibid.
11. Liz Smith quoted in Betsy von Furstenberg's column "My Side," *Working Women,* September 1982, p. 20.
12. Barbara Ehrenreich, "Feminist Notes: The 'Playboy' Man and the American Family," *Ms.,* June 1983, p. 14.
13. "The Myth of Equality," NOW (National Organization of Women) promotional material, 1983, and *Working Woman,* July 1980, pp. 27–29. Some statistics from *The Coming Matriarchy* by Elizabeth Nickles with Laura Ashcraft (New York: Berkeley, 1982), pp. 141–143.
14. Ehrenreich, "Feminist Notes: The 'Playboy' Man and the American Family," p. 16.
15. Eckhardt, "Exchange in Sexual Permissiveness"; see also Robert Staples, "The New Sex vs. The Old Ideals," *Essence,* May 1981, p. 83.
16. Ehrenreich, "Feminist Notes: The 'Playboy' Man and the American Family," p. 16.

3: CROSSED WIRES, MIXED MESSAGES

1. e. e. cummings' poem from *Complete Poems, 1913–1962* (New York: Harcourt Brace Jovanovich, 1972).
2. Quote from Carol Tavris and Carole Offir, *The Longest War* (New York: Harcourt Brace Jovanovich, 1977), p. 69.
3. Statistics taken from Anthony Pietropinto and Jacqueline Simenauer, *Beyond the Male Myth* (New York: Signet, 1977), p. 230.
4. Shere Hite, *The Hite Report on Male Sexuality* (New York: Ballantine Books, 1982), p. xiv.
5. From *Dialectic of Sex* (New York: Bantam Books, 1972), p. 127.
6. Pietropinto and Simenauer, *Beyond the Male Myth,* p. 239.
7. This is from a study of 400 unmarried undergraduate women attending a large southeastern university during the spring of 1979: Sheila K. Korman and Gerald R. Leslie, "The Relationship of Feminist Ideology and Date Expense Sharing to Perceptions of Sexual Aggression in Dating," *Journal of Sex Research,* 18, 2 (May 1982), 114–129.
8. Corby Kummer, "The Unsinkable Lauren Bacall," *McCalls,* May 1981, p. 68.

9. "What Does a Woman Need? Not to Depend upon a Man," *People*, September 13, 1982, p. 75. Russianoff was being interviewed in conjunction with her new book, *Why Do I Think I Am Nothing Without a Man?* (New York: Bantam Books, 1982).

10. Linda Blocki, "Decoding Manspeak," *Albuquerque Singles Scene*, May 1982, p. 11. Also, she discusses the commitment phobia epidemic in "Fear of Commitment," *Albuquerque Singles Scene*, August 1981.

11. For a readable examination of the Masters and Johnson's physiology studies, with accurate social and historical perspectives, see Edward and Ruth Brecher, *An Analysis of Human Sexual Response* (New York: New American Library, 1966).

12. Scene from Daisy Maryless and Robert Dahlin, eds., "Special Report: The World of Romance Fiction," *Publishers Weekly*, 1982, p. 23.

13. William H. Masters, Virginia E. Johnson, and Robert C. Koloday, *Human Sexuality* (Boston: Little, Brown, 1982), pp. 55–80. Material on the physiological responses of the brain from Jo Durden-Smith and Diane deSimone, *Sex and the Brain* (New York: Arbor House, 1983), Chapters 15–18.

14. Dr. Liebowitz's work reported by Glenn Collins, "Chemical Connections: Pathways of Love," *The New York Times*, February 14, 1982. For other information on the chemical connections between the brain and our sexual feelings see Durden-Smith and deSimone, *Sex and the Brain*.

15. Ann Barr Snitow, "Sex in Novels," *Women, Sex and Sexuality* (Chicago: University of Chicago Press, 1980), p. 162.

16. Dorothy Parker quoted in Tavris and Offir, *The Longest War*, p. 60.

17. Study from S. Gordon, P. Scales, and K. Everly, *The Sexual Adolescent* (North Scituate, Mass.: Duxbury Press, 1979), p. 58.

18. William M. Kephart, "Some Correlates of Romantic Love," *Journal of Marriage and the Family*, 29, 3 (1967), 470–474.

19. Kenneth Z. Dion and Karen K. Dion, "Correlates of Romantic Love," *Journal of Consulting Clinical Psychology*, 41, 1 (August 1973), 51–56. See also Harvey Black and Virginia B. Angelis, "Interpersonal Attraction: An Empirical Investigation of Platonic and Romantic Love," *Psychological Reports*, 34, 30 (June 1974), 1243–1246; James Dretch, "Love, Sex Roles and Psychological Health," *Journal of Personality Assessment*, 42, 6 (December 1978), 626–634; and Robert J. Morais and Allen L. Tan, "Male-Female Differences

in Conceptions of Romantic Love Relationships," *Psychological Reports*, 47(3P-12) (December 1980), 1221–1222.

20. Bryan Strong, Sam Wilson, Leah Miller Clarke, and Thomas John, *Human Sexuality: The Essentials* (St. Paul, Minn.: West Publishing Co., 1978), p. 19.

21. Statistical survey by McCormick from "Dating Rituals," *Human Behavior*, August 1978, p. 67.

22. Carol Robert's research reported in Tavris and Offir, *The Longest War*, pp. 67–69.

23. David Shope, *Interpersonal Sexuality* (Philadelphia: W. B. Saunders Co., 1975), p. 35.

24. Ira Reiss is quoted in Shope, *Interpersonal Sexuality*, p. 36.

25. Robert Hazo is quoted in Shope, *Interpersonal Sexuality*, p. 40.

26. Stendhal, quoted in "The Joys of Love," *McCalls*, February 1982, p. 74.

27. Robert Solomon, "The Love Lost in Clichés," *Psychology Today*, October 1981, p. 84.

28. Soloman, "The Love Lost in Clichés," p. 83.

29. Charlie Brown quote from Pietropinto and Simenauer, *Beyond the Male Myth*, p. 225.

4: STILL GOOD GIRLS AFTER ALL THESE YEARS

1. Greer Litton Fox provides outstanding insight into society's need to keep women Good Girls in "Nice Girls: Social Control of Women Through Value Construct," *Signs*, 2 (1977). Other material on "Good Girls" taken from Germaine Greer, *The Female Eunuch* (New York: Bantam Books, 1972), pp. 1–12; Nancy Friday, *My Mother/My Self*, Chapter 9, "The Loss of Virginity"; Leslie A. Fiedler, "Good Girls and Bad Boys, Clarissa As a Juvenile," *Love and Death in the American Novel* (New York: Stein and Day, 1966). For conditioning of "Good Girls," Colette Dowling, *The Cinderella Complex* (New York: Summit Books, 1981), provides a look at how parents (with good intentions) code submissive behavior into females and steer them into an "I'm not responsible" course. See also Madonna Kolbenschlag, *Kiss Sleeping Beauty Goodbye* (New York: Bantam Books, 1981).

2. Quote from Greer Litton Fox, "Nice Girls," p. 810.

3. Masters and Johnson quoted in Janet Harris, *The Prime of Ms. America* (New York: New American Library, 1976), p. 85.

4. Ray E. Short, *Sex, Love or Infatuation* (Minneapolis: Augsburg 1978), Chapter 10, "To Be or Not to Be—A Virgin." See also "Marie Osmond Still Saying No!" *Ladies' Home Journal,* March 1982, p. 45. See the National Clearinghouse for Family Planning Information, Health Education Bulletin, "Counseling for Teens: The Consequences of Sexual Activity," June 1981, No. 22. The back cover shouts, "WHAT HAPPENS WHEN YOU HAVE INTERCOURSE: . . . Lots of teens wonder about that, and here's what happened when they had intercourse:

- 8 in 10 dropped out of high school
- 6 in 10 who married were divorced in five years
- 7 in 10 went on welfare
- their income was a whopping $7,500 a year
- their babies are twice as likely to die as other babies
- they are more than twice as likely to die themselves during pregnancy."

Ad for *Heartbreak U.S.A.* was in *The New York Times,* April 10, 1983.
5. "Menstruation Still Taboo Subject," *Sexuality Today,* July 13, 1981, p. 3. Also, *Dallas Times,* August 23, 1981.
6. "Dear Abby," New York *Daily News,* May 15, 1982.
7. First quote is from Signe Hammer's *Daughters and Mothers, Mothers and Daughters* in Kolbenschlag's *Kiss Sleeping Beauty Goodbye,* p. 40. Also see p. 41. For a view of how we are locked into the two worlds of generations see Janet Harris, *The Prime of Ms. America.*
8. From *The Cosmo Report* (New York: Arbor House, 1981), p. 157. Author Linda Wolfe says: "The majority of the women have had numerous lovers. The median was nine lovers per woman, with 10 percent of the women having had only one and 15 percent having had more than 25. The exact breakdown was: one lover: 10 percent; two to five lovers: 28 percent; eleven to twenty-five lovers: 25 percent; twenty-five or more lovers: 15 percent." Wolfe adds, "No other figures yielded by the *Cosmo* Sex Survey seem as much a revelation as these. Indeed, in an important sense, the sexual revolution can be characterized as today's widespread practice of picking and choosing among lovers. And the number of partners a woman of today is likely to pick and choose is, frankly, stunning."

9. Three excellent sources are Dowling, *The Cinderella Complex;* Tavris and Offir, *The Longest War;* and Caryl Rivers, Rosalind Barnett, and Grace Baruch, *Beyond Sugar and Spice* (New York: Ballantine Books, 1979).
10. "Sex: Blinking at the Birds and Bees," *Human Behavior,* February 1979, p. 58, about a study of sex education practices of 124 California mothers.
11. Friday, *My Mother/My Self,* p. 102.
12. R. J. Levin, "The Redbook Report on Premarital and Extramarital Sex," *Redbook,* October 1975, pp. 38–44, 190. See also McCary, *Human Sexuality,* 3rd ed., pp. 252–255.
13. Fox, "Nice Girl," p. 809.
14. Ibid., p. 811.
15. Friday, *My Mother/My Self,* p. 275.
16. George Carlin's quote from his record album *Class Clown,* Little David Records, 1972, the section called "I used to be Irish Catholic."
17. The scandal was this: In 1950 Ingrid Bergman left her husband Dr. Peter Lindstrom to live with (unmarried!) Roberto Rossellini. Before long the news was out that she was pregnant by Rossellini and within six months or so gave birth to a son named Roberto. Two years later she had twin girls. In 1954 she married Rossellini when her divorce was final from Lindstrom. Then she and Rossellini got divorced in 1957. But from 1950 to 1954 their lives were front-page news, and she was considered to be a "fallen woman."
18. Elizabeth Janeway, *Between Myth and Morning: Women Awakening* (New York: William Morrow, 1975), p. 9.

5: LEARNING THE RULES

1. A. C. Kinsey, W. B. Pomeroy, C. E. Martin, and H. P. Gebhard, *Sexual Behavior in the Human Female* (Philadelphia: Saunders, 1953). Premarital sex statistics from Levin, "The Redbook Report on Premarital and Extramarital Sex," pp. 38–44, 190.
2. Ira Reiss is the researcher who found this change in sexual behavior; see *SIECUS* report, "Premarital Sexual Standards," Study Guide No. 5 (revised), 1975. John Fluegel quoted in Theo Lang, *The Difference Between a Man and a Woman* (New York: Bantam Books, 1973), p. 191.

3. Information on males' use of prostitutes from McCary, *Human Sexuality*, 2nd Brief Edition (New York: Van Nostrand, 1979), p. 168.

4. Quote from "The Seventies and How We Got Away with It," *New York*, December 31, 1979/January 7, 1980, p. 34. 1976-1985 declared by United Nations as Decade for Women, Equality, Development and Peace.

5. Statistics from Levin, "The Redbook Report on Premarital and Extramarital Sex," and Kinsey et al., *Sexual Behavior in the Human Female*. Changes in teenage sex behavior from M. Zelnick and J. F. Kanter, "Sexual and Contraceptive Experience of Young Unmarried Women in the United States, 1976 and 1971," *Family Planning Perspectives*, 9, 2, 1978. Report on attitude polls of University of Chicago's National Opinion Research Center in David Fink, "The Sexes Agree More About Sex," *USA Today*, July 10, 1983, p. 1, and "The Sexual Revolution," *Ladies' Home Journal*, May 1982, p. 88.

6. Barbara Ehrenreich, Elizabeth Hess, and Gloria Jacobs, "A Report on the Sex Crisis," *Ms.*, March 1982, p. 61.

7. See Marie Richmond-Abbott and Nadean Bishop, "The New Old-Fashioned Womanhood," *Human Behavior*, April 1977. The authors review a cluster of books aimed at combating women's liberation.

8. Quote from "The Way We Were—And Will Be," *Ms.*, December 1979, p. 60.

9. For an in-depth review of historical reasons for virginity see Herant Katchadourian and Donald Lunde, *Fundamentals of Human Sexuality*, 2nd ed. (New York: Holt, Rinehart and Winston, 1975), pp. 539, 548–552.

10. From Pietropinto and Simenauer, *Beyond the Male Myth*, pp. 207–209. "Virgins were most threatening to the divorced/widowed and those living with a partner (20 percent for both). Older men were more at ease with them than the younger, having been acquainted with them long before they became an endangered species. Nonwhites (19 percent) were less at ease with virgins than whites (13 percent). Highly educated men were more threatened by virgins; only 9 percent of men without high school diplomas cited virgins as anxiety-provoking, against 16 percent of postgraduate men."

11. Lang, *The Difference Between a Man and a Woman*, p. 191.

12. Pietropinto and Simenauer, *Beyond the Male Myth*, p. 296.

6: THE REVOLUTIONARY FAÇADE

1. From "Marrying, Divorcing, and Living Together in the U.S. Today," *Population Bulletin*, 32, 5 (February 1979). "Marital Status and Living Arrangements," U.S. Bureau of the Census Current Population Reports, Series P-20, No. 365 (Washington, D.C.: U.S. Government Printing Office, 1981). "Family and Marriage Statistics," *Vital Statistics*, 32, 5 (Supplement), August 1983. Also Orland Thorton and Deborah Freedman, "The Changing American Family," *Population Reference Bureau*, 34, 4 October 1983.

2. McCary, *Human Sexuality*, 3rd ed., pp. 243–248.

3. Harris, *The Prime of Ms. America*, p. 35.

4. Ehrenreich, Hess, and Jacobs, "A Report on the Sex Crisis," *Ms.*, March 1982, p. 60.

5. Shere Hite, *The Hite Report* (New York: Dell, 1976), pp. 448. This is one of the most important sources of information about how women really feel about sex.

6. Ibid., pp. 479–484.

7. Masters and Johnson quoted in Harris, *The Prime of Ms. America*, p. 76.

8. Jacqueline Swartz, "How to Live with—and Love—a Semi-Liberated Man," *New Dawn*, July 1977, p. 54.

9. Figures on male/female ratio from U.S. Census, *Statistical Abstract of the U.S.*, 1980, and from "Divorce," *Albuquerque Singles Scene*, November 1982. See also Jones, *Great Expectations*, pp. 208–213, for a clear explanation of how the "marriage squeeze" developed. And for one of the best reviews and analyses of why men are less available for women who want marriage read Barbara Ehrenreich's *The Heart of Men* (New York: Doubleday Anchor, 1983).

10. Novak in an interview by Judy Foreman, "A Good, Single Man Gets Harder to Find," *Boston Globe*, October 18, 1981, p. 21.

11. Swartz, "How to Live with—and Love—A Semi-Liberated Man," p. 54.

12. This research was published in 1982; see Alice Ladas, Beverly Whipple, and John Perry, *The G-Spot* (New York: Holt, Rinehart and Winston, 1982).

13. The Sarrels are quoted by Kathleen Fury in "Sex and the American Teenager," *Ladies' Home Journal*, April 1980.

14. Nathaniel Wagner, ed. *Perspectives on Human Sexuality*. New York: Behavioral Publications, 1974, p. ix.

15. Wolfe, *The Cosmo Report*. p. xxiv and p. 256.

16. George Bach and Laura Torbet, "Caring In and Out of Bed," *Redbook*, April 1982, p. 82.

7: ROMANCE—RENAISSANCE OR REGRESSION?

1. Bill Abrams, "Why Revlon's Charlie Seems to Be Ready to Settle Down," *The Wall Street Journal*, December 23, 1982, p. 11.
2. Trends toward more traditional relationships reported in "The Sexual Revolution," *Ladies' Home Journal*, May 1982, p. 88. Also the results of the NBC/AP poll were discussed in this article.
3. Rivers, Barnett, and Baruch, *Beyond Sugar and Spice*, p. 167.
4. Women's employment aspirations from Virginia Slims Poll of 1980 as reported in "Today's American Woman: How the Public Sees Her," prepared for the President's Advisory Committee for Women by the Public Agenda Foundation. Investigators were Deborah Durfee Barron and Daniel Yankelovich, September 1980. See the survey in *USA Today*, "Marriage Outranks a Career," *USA Today*, October 5, 1988.
5. Students' attitudes about family and careers from "Right Now," *McCalls*, May 1981, pp. 37–38.
6. Dowling, *The Cinderella Complex*, p. 31.
7. Barbara Lazear Ascher, "Hers," a column in *The New York Times*, February 3, 1983.
8. Christine Terp Madsen, "Teen Books: Promoting the 'Right' Values?" *The Christian Science Monitor*, January 7, 1982, p. B-8. Also, Elizabeth Mehren, "Young Girls Still Looking for Prince Charming," Syracuse *Post-Standard*, May 16, 1983, p. A-7.
9. William E. Geist, "Weddings Flourish Today," *The New York Times*, May 18, 1982.
10. Greer, *The Female Eunuch*, p. 227. A good example of how we make up the characteristics for the Prince Charming we want so badly and what happens when he fails to live up to our fantasy is in Gary Michael Durst, *Napkin Notes: On the Art of Living* (Chicago: The Center for the Art of Living, 1980), pp. 136, 193.
11. Jan Hoffman, "Making Up Is Hard to Do," *Village Voice*, May 31, 1983.
12. Robert Sanchez, "Sex—How Sex Appeal Is Used as an Attention Getter," *New Mexico Daily Lobo*, April 2, 1982, p. R-1.
13. Maryless and Dahlin, "Special Report: The World of Romance Fiction."
14. From a mimeographed tip sheet sent to hopeful writers.

15. Patricia O'Toole, "Paperback Virgins," *Human Behavior*, February 1979, pp. 63–67.
16. Maryless and Dahlin, "Special Report: The World of Romance Fiction."
17. From "Paperback Talk," *The New York Times Book Review*, February 13, 1983.
18. Review by Gene Siskel, "American Salutes an Officer and a Gentleman," *Albuquerque Journal*, December 5, 1982, Sec. D, p. 1.

8: GOOD GIRLS AND BAD CONTRACEPTION

1. See data in *Understanding Your Body*, 1988, especially Chapter 11, "Choosing a Method of Birth Control," and the article, "The Characteristics and Prior Contraceptive Use of U.S. Abortion Patients," 1988. A 1983 analysis of 1978 data found most sexually active women do successfully avoid unwanted pregnancy, about 27.1 million out of 37.1 million sexually active and fertile women. But still, out of the total group 4.4 million got unintentionally pregnant; a slightly lesser number, 4.1 million, had a planned pregnancy, and another 1.5 million tried but failed to get pregnant. What is important to know, though, is that out of the 27.1 million women who avoided pregnancy, 24 percent had been sterilized; 40 percent used the Pill or the IUD; 21 percent used a barrier method; 7 percent were dependent upon rhythm, withdrawal, or douching; and 8 percent used nothing at all. See Joy G. Dryfoos' article "Contraceptive Use, Pregnancy Intentions and Pregnancy Outcomes Among U.S. Women," *Family Planning Perspectives*, 2 (March-April 1983), 52–111; and Allen L. Schirm, James Trussell, Jane Menken, and William Grady, "Contraceptive Failure in the United States: The Impact of Social, Economic and Demographic Factors" in the same issue. The findings of the latter study using 1976 data are that the failure rates are lowest with the Pill and highest with rhythm for women in each age, income, and intention category. Women over twenty-five, but not younger women, are more successful at preventing pregnancy. Poor young women have little success using any method except the Pill or IUD.

For the statistics on married women see "U.S. Women's Contraceptive Attitudes and Practice: How Have They Changed in the 1980s?", *Family Planning Perspectives*, 20, 3 (May-June 1988), 112. For abortion statistics see "Abortion Surveillance Annual

Summary 1978," *The Centers for Disease Control,* Atlanta, Ga.: Public Health Service, November 1980.

2. Robert A. Hatcher, M.D., Gary K. Stewart, M.D., et al, *Contraceptive Technology 1986–1987* (New York: John Wiley & Sons, 1987).

3. See Dryfoos, "Contraceptive Use, Pregnancy Intentions and Pregnancy Outcomes Among U.S. Women"; S. Marie Harvey, "Trends in Contraceptive Use at One University: 1974–1978," *Family Planning Perspectives,* 12 (November-December 1980), 301–304; Richard H. Needle, "Factors Affecting Contraceptive Practices of High School and College-Age Students," *Journal of School Health,* June 1977, pp. 340–344; W. A. Fisher, D. Byrne, J. Edmunds, C. Miller, K. Kelley, L. White, "Psychological and Situation-Specific Correlates of Contraception Behavior Among University Women," *Journal of Sex Research,* 15, 1 (1979), 38–55.

4. Kristin Luker, "The Male Role in Family Planning," Conference Proceedings, June 1977, Office of Family Planning, California Department of Health, p. 14. Luker's major theory deals with why women, knowing they could get pregnant, still take a chance and do not use birth control. She states that women weigh the costs of using birth control versus the cost of getting pregnant. Many then decide they would rather risk getting pregnant than putting themselves on the spot by using contraception. "Another aspect of the theory of decision making under conditions of risk defines the difference between 'risk' and 'uncertainty,' a difference that plays a significant part in women's decisions to take risks with contraception. In classical decision-making theory, a 'risk' is a probability of known magnitude: there is a consensus as to the likelihood of a given event. An 'uncertainty,' on the other hand, is a probability of unknown magnitude. Thus for women, getting pregnant is an 'uncertainty.' " Quoted from Luker's *Taking Chances,* p. 36.

   For another view of Luker's theory of contraceptive risk-taking, see Paul V. Crosbie and Dianne Bitte, "A Test of Luker's Theory of Contraceptive Risk-Taking," *Studies in Family Planning,* 13, 3 (March 1982), 67–76. They say that "the theory has wide appeal but has yet to be empirically confirmed."

5. Lowry, "Unwanted Pregnancy—Why?"

6. Fox, "Nice Girl," p. 816.

7. Elizabeth Roberts in "Sexuality and Social Policy: The Unwritten Curriculum," *Childhood Sexual Learning* (Cambridge, Mass.: Ballinger, 1980), p. 275.

8. Pamela Rains, *Becoming an Unwed Mother* (Chicago: Aldine, 1971). For a good review of her study see John Delamater and Patricia Maccorguodale, "Premarital Contraceptive Use: A Test of Two Models," *Journal of Marriage and the Family*, 23 (May 1978,) p. 23.

9. Encare ad in *Ms.*, March 1982, p. 65.

10. Sol Gordon's comments from his lecture given at the Institute for Family Research and Education, July 13, 1981, at Thornfield Summer Session.

11. NAB survey cited in Patricia Donovan, "Airing Contraceptive Commercials," *Family Planning Perspectives*, 14, 6 (November-December 1982), 321–323.

12. McCary, *Human Sexuality*, 2nd Brief Edition, p. 5, in chapter entitled "Sex and Today's Society."

13. Edward Pohlman, *The Psychology of Birth Planning* (Cambridge, Mass.: Schenkeman, 1969), p. 353. His observations have held up over time.

14. Marian L. Upchurch, "Sex Guilt and Contraceptive Use," *Journal of Sex Education and Therapy*, 4, 1 (Spring/Summer 1978), 27–30. See also Edward Herold and Marilyn Goodwin, "Premarital Sexual Guilt and Contraceptive Attitudes and Behavior," *Family Relations*, 30 April 1981. This includes a very thorough review of current research on this topic.

15. Information about theories from Gordon E. Rader, L. DeMoyne Bekker, Laura Brown, and Cheryl Richardt, "Psychological Correlates of Unwanted Pregnancy," paper presented at Annual Convention of the American Psychological Association, San Francisco, August 26, 1977; and from Luker, *Taking Chances*. See also William B. Miller, "Psychological Vulnerability to Unwanted Pregnancy," *Family Planning Perspectives*, 5, 4 (1975), 199–201.

16. Michael Bracken, Lorraine Klerman, and Maryann Bracken, "Coping with Pregnancy Resolution Among Never-Married Women," *American Journal of Orthopsychiatry*, 48, 2 (April 1978), 328.

17. Carol Cassell, "In Perspective: Male Involvement," *Emphasis*, Summer 1981, published by Education Department of the Planned Parenthood Federation of America.

18. Depo-Provera is a progesterone-like synthetic compound. One injection prevents ovulation for at least three months. The sponge is a soft, disposable polyurethane substance. Efficiency rates vary. This figure of 85 percent comes from the FDA. See Joseph

Lederer, "Birth-Control Decisions," *Psychology Today*, June 1983, pp. 32–38.

9: MEN TALK/MAN TALK

1. Nancy Friday quoted in Larry Miller, "Man/Woman Desire: Devastating Differences," *Cosmopolitan*, July 1982, p. 263.
2. Janeway, *Man's World, Woman's Place*, p. 203. See also Naomi B. McCormick, "Dating Rituals," *Human Behavior*, August 1979, p. 67. McCormick found that "both traditional and profeminist [university] students continue to expect a sexual dating script in which the male attempts to gain access to the female's body and the female either passively accepts the male's advances or actively blocks his efforts."
3. Dan Greenburg, *Scoring* (New York: Doubleday, 1972), pp. 9–12.
4. Jessie Bernard, *The Sex Game* (Englewood Cliffs, N.J.: Prentice-Hall, 1968), pp. 93–94. See also Nancy Friday's excellent discussion of sex, power, and women in *My Mother/My Self*, pp. 318–319.
5. Janeway, *Man's World, Woman's Place*, p. 198.
6. Farrell, "Risking Sexual Rejection: Women's Last Frontier?" p. 100.
7. Robert Staples, "The New Sex vs. The Old Ideals," *Essence*, May 1981, p. 83. For another outstanding point of view on sex and power see Uta West, "The Politics of Courtship," *Working Women*, March 1982, p. 100.
8. Bernard, *The Sex Game*, p. 89.
9. David Bradley, "A Man Explains Why I Said 'I'll Call You' and Didn't," *Savoy*, December 1980, pp. 36–37. I received *nine* copies of this article from friends who knew I was planning to write a book that included women's disappointment with men in the post-sexual revolution. I had comments ranging from "What about old-fashioned manners?" to "So the S.O.B.'s try to explain!" See also *Glamour*, July 1982, information on Jacqueline Simenauer and David Carroll's book *Singles*, in which they reported the following:

Why Doesn't He Call Again?	*Men*
I find her dull and superficial.	30%
She is immature or neurotic.	20%

It's usually my way to go out with a woman
    a few times and then move on.   15%
She loses interest.   12%
She presses me too quickly for
    intimacy and involvement.   10%
She refuses to have sex   6%
Don't know.   5%
She is a poor lover.   3%

The best source of what has happened to men's ideas of commitment is Barbara Ehrenreich, *The Hearts of Men*. For a clear explanation of why a man may not continue a relationship see Daniel
Goldstine, Katherine Larner, Shirley Zucherman, and Hilary
Goldstine, *The Dance-Away Lover* (New York: Ballantine Books,
1978).
10. Susan Locke quoted in Georgia Dullea, "Relationships: Marriage
versus Living Together," *The New York Times*, February 14, 1983.
For more information on men's dual conditioning toward women
see Pietropinto and Simenauer, *Beyond the Male Myth*, Chapter 12,
the section called "The Saintly Prostitute"; Kohlbenschlag, *Kiss
Sleeping Beauty Goodbye*, pp. 174–175; and Harris, *The Prime of Ms.
America*, Chapter 3, "One of the Girls."
11. Daniel Yankelovich quoted in Marilyn Machlowetz's column in
Working Women, March 1982, p. 111.
12. Tom McGuane quoted in "The New Appeal of Women-
Strength," *Self*, July 1982, pp. 55–56.
13. Michael Carrera quoted in Larry Miller, "Man/Woman Desires:
Devastating Differences," *Cosmopolitan*, July 1982. See also Michael Castleman, *Sexual Solutions* (New York: Simon and Schuster, 1980). For information on the change in male roles and the
difficulty men have in making these changes see William J.
Goode, ed., "Why Men Resist," *Rethinking the Family* (New York:
Thorne, 1978), pp. 131–150.
14. Michael Korda, "Sexual Bargaining," *Self*, February 1982.

10: INVENTING YOURSELF

1. Rayna Rapp, quoted in "A Report on the Sex Crisis," *Ms.*, March
1982, p. 87.
 2. Alex Comfort, quoted in *SIECUS* report, "Premarital Sexual Standards," Study Guide No. 5 (revised, 1975), p. 26.

3. Jill Conway, "A Proper Perspective," in *Today's Girls, Tomorrow's Women* (New York: Girls Club of America, 1980), p. 16.

4. Carin Rubenstein, "The Modern Art of Courtly Love," *Psychology Today*, July 1983, p. 44.

5. Farrell, "Risking Sexual Rejection: Women's Last Frontier?" p. 100.

6. Ad from *Village Voice*, July 15, 1982, p. 47.

7. Anthony Brandt, "We're Equals, But I'm the Boss," *McCall's*, August 1983, p. 72.

8. Ibid. See also Goode, "Why Men Resist."

9. Statistics from Wolfe, *The Cosmo Report.*

10. Personal interview, September 1982.

11. Barbara Seaman, author of *Free and Female*, quoted in "The New Morality," *Time*, January 1977, p. 15.

12. Carol Callahan, "How Sex Without Commitment Can Be Good for Your Ego," *Woman*, June 1982, pp. 6–7.

13. *Safe Encounters: How Women Can Say Yes to Pleasure and No to Unsafe Sex* is a terrific book offering women a responsible and balanced approach to promoting safer sex—as opposed to uncertainty or fear—in the wake of the AIDS epidemic. For more information, call The National AIDS Clearinghouse (1-800-458-5231).

14. Sheri Tepper, *So You Don't Want to Be a Sex Object* (Denver, Colo.: Rocky Mountain Planned Parenthood, 1973), pp. 4–7.

15. Elizabeth Nickles with Laura Ashcraft, *The Coming Matriarchy: How Women Will Gain the Balance of Power* (New York: Berkley Books, 1982), p. 147.

BIBLIOGRAPHY

BOOKS

Baer, Jean. *How to Be an Assertive (Not Aggressive) Woman in Life, in Love, and on the Job.* New York: New American Library, 1976.

Bernard, Jessie. *The Sex Game.* Englewood Cliffs, N.J.: Prentice-Hall, 1968.

Brecher, Edward, and Ruth Brecher. *Analysis of Human Sexual Response.* New York: New American Library, 1966.

Brothers, Joyce, M.D. *What Every Woman Should Know About Men.* New York: Simon and Schuster, 1981.

Calderone, Mary, and Eric Johnson. *The Family Book About Sensuality.* New York: Harper and Row, 1981.

Carrera, Michael. *Sex—The Facts, the Acts, and Your Feelings.* New York: Crown Publishers, 1981.

Cartland, Barbara. *Dreams Do Come True.* New York: Bantam Books, 1981.

Castleman, Michael. *Sexual Solutions: An Informative Guide.* New York: Simon and Schuster, 1980.

cummings, e. e. *Complete Poems: 1913–1962.* New York: Harcourt Brace Jovanovich, 1972.

Dowling, Colette. *The Cinderella Complex: Women's Hidden Fear of Independence.* New York: Summit Books, 1981.

Druck, Dr. Ken, with James C. Simmons. *The Secrets Men Keep.* New York: Ballantine Books, 1987.

Durden-Smith, Jo, and Diane deSimone. *Sex and the Brain.* New York: Arbor House. 1983.

Durst, Gary Michael. *Napkin Notes: On the Art of Living.* Chicago: Center for the Art of Living, 1980.

Ehrenreich, Barbara. *The Hearts of Men.* New York: Doubleday/Anchor, 1983.

Ehrenreich, Barbara, Elizabeth Hess, and Gloria Jacobs. *Re-Making Love: The Feminization of Sex.* Garden City, New York: Anchor Press/ Doubleday, 1986.

Ephron, Nora. *Crazy Salad.* New York: Bantam Books, 1980.

Farrell, Warren, Ph.D. *Why Men Are the Way They Are.* New York: McGraw-Hill, 1986.

Fiedler, Leslie A. "Good Good Girls and Good Bad Boys, Clarissa as a Juvenile." In *Love and Death in the American Novel.* New York: Stein and Day, 1966.

Filene, Peter. *Him, Her, Self: Sex Roles in Modern America.* New York: Harcourt Brace Jovanovich, 1974.

Firestone, Shulamith. *Dialectic of Sex.* New York: Bantam Books, 1972.

Friday, Nancy. *My Mother/My Self: The Daughter's Search for Identity.* New York: Delacorte Press, 1977.

Friday, Nancy. *Jealousy.* New York: William Morrow, 1985.

Friedan, Betty. *The Feminine Mystique.* New York: Bantam Books, 1973.

———. *The Second Stage.* New York: Summit Books, 1981.

Goffman, Irving, ed. "The Arrangement Between the Sexes," *Theory and Society.* Amsterdam: Elsevier Scientific Publishing Co., 1977.

Goldstine, Daniel, Katherine Larner, Shirley Zucherman, and Hilary Goldstine. *The Dance-Away Lover.* New York: Ballantine Books, 1978.

Goode, William J., ed. "Why Men Resist." In *Rethinking the Family.* New York: Thorne, 1978.

Gordon, Sol, Peter Scales, and Kathleen Everly. *The Sexual Adolescent: Communicating with Teenagers About Sex.* 2nd ed. North Scituate, Mass.: Duxbury Press, 1979.

Gordon, Sol. *Why Love Is Not Enough.* Boston: Bob Adams, Inc., 1988.

Greer, Germaine. *The Female Eunuch.* New York: Bantam Books, 1972.

Hanson, Dian. *How to Pick Up a Man.* New York: G. P. Putnam's Sons, 1982. Don't let the title put you off; this is an excellent book— down-to-earth advice.

Harris, Janet. *The Prime of Ms. America.* New York: New American Library, 1976.

Hatcher, Robert A., M.D., Felicia Stewart, M.D., Gary K. Stewart, M.D., Felicia Guest, et al. *Contraceptive Technology 1986–1987.* New York: John Wiley and Sons, 1987.

Hatfield, E., M. Utne, and J. Traupmann. "Equity Theory and Intimate Relationships," in R. Burgess and T. L. Huston (eds.), *Social Exchange in Developing Relationships.* New York: Academic Press, 1979.

Heimel, Cynthia. *Sex Tips for Girls.* New York: Simon and Schuster, 1983.

Hite, Shere. *The Hite Report: A Nationwide Study of Female Sexuality.* New York: Dell Books, 1977.

Hite, Shere. *The Hite Report of Male Sexuality.* New York: Ballantine Books, 1981.

Hite, Shere. *Women and Love: A Cultural Revolution in Progress.* New York: Alfred A. Knopf, 1987.

Janeway, Elizabeth. *Between Myth and Morning: Women Awakening.* New York: William Morrow, 1975.

————. *Man's World, Woman's Place: A Study in Social Mythology.* New York: Dell, 1970.

Jones, Landon Y. *Great Expectations: America and the Baby Boom Generation.* New York: Ballantine Books, 1980.

Katchadourian, Herant A., and Donald A. Lunde. *Fundamentals of Human Sexuality.* 2nd ed. New York: Holt, Rinehart and Winston, 1975.

Kinsey, A. C., W. B. Pomeroy, C. E. Martin, and H. P. Gebhard. *Sexual Behavior in the Human Female.* Philadelphia: Saunders, 1953.

Kolbenschlag, Madonna. *Kiss Sleeping Beauty Goodbye.* New York: Bantam Books, 1981.

Ladas, Alice, Beverly Whipple, and John Perry. *The G-Spot.* New York: Holt, Rinehart and Winston, 1982.

Lang, Theo. *The Difference Between a Man and a Woman.* New York: Bantam Books, 1973.

Ledere, Wolfgang. *The Fear of Women.* New York: Harcourt Brace Jovanovich, 1968.

Luker, Kristin. *Taking Chances: Abortion and the Decision Not to Contracept.* Berkeley, Calif.: University of California Press, 1978.

Martin, M. Kay, and Barbara Voorhies. *Female of the Species.* New York: Columbia University Press, 1975.

Masters, William H., Virginia E. Johnson, and Robert C. Koloday. *Human Sexuality.* Boston: Little, Brown, 1982.

May, Rollo. *Love and Will.* New York: Delta, 1969.

McCary, James. *Human Sexuality.* 2nd Brief Edition. New York: Van Nostrand, 1979; 3rd ed., 1978.

Nickles, Elizabeth, with Laura Ashcraft. *The Coming Matriarchy: How Women Will Gain the Balance of Power.* New York: Berkley, 1982.

Peter, Laurence J. *Peter's Quotations: Ideas for Our Time.* New York: William Morrow, 1977.

Pietropinto, Anthony, M.D., and Jacqueline Simenauer. *Beyond the Male Myth.* New York: Signet, 1977.

Pogrebin, Letty Cottin. *Growing Up Free.* New York: Bantam Books 1980.

Pohlman, Edward, *The Psychology of Birth Planning.* Cambridge, Mass.: Schenkeman, 1969.

Rivers, Caryl, Rosalind Barnett, and Grace Baruch. *Beyond Sugar and Spice.* New York: Ballantine Books, 1979.

Roberts, Elizabeth J., ed. *Childhood Sexual Learning: The Unwritten Curriculum.* Cambridge, Mass.: Ballinger, 1980.

Roszak, Betty, and Theodore Roszak, eds. *Masculine/Feminine: Readings in Sexual Mythology and the Liberation of Women.* New York: Harper and Row, 1969.

Sanday, Peggy Reeves. *Female Power and Male Dominance.* Boston: Cambridge University Press, 1981.

Shaine, Merle. *When Lovers Are Friends.* New York: Bantam Books, 1980.

Shope, David F. *Interpersonal Sexuality.* Philadelphia: W. B. Saunders Co., 1975.

Short, Ray E. *Sex, Love or Infatuation.* Minneapolis: Augsburg, 1978.

Stewart, Felicia, M.D., Felicia Guest, Gary Stewart, M.D., and Robert Hatcher, M.D. *Understanding Your Body: Every Woman's Guide to Gynecology and Health.* New York: Bantam Books, 1987.

Stimpson, Catharine, and Ethel Spector Pearson, eds. *Women: Sex and Sexuality.* Chicago: University of Chicago Press, 1980.

Strong, Bryan, et al. *Human Sexuality: Essentials.* St. Paul, Minn.: West Publishing Co., 1978.

Tannahill, Reay. *Sex in History.* New York: Stein and Day, 1980.

Tavris, Carol, and Carole Offir. *The Longest War: Sex Differences in Perspective.* New York: Harcourt Brace Jovanovich, 1977.

Tunnadine, David, and Roger Green. *Unwanted Pregnancy—Accident or Illness?* New York: Oxford University Press, 1978.

von Franz, Marie-Louise. *Problems of the Feminine in Fairytales.* Irving, Texas: Spring Publications, 1972.

Wagner, Nathaniel. *Perspectives on Human Sexuality.* New York: Behavioral Publications, 1974.

Whipple, Beverly, Ph.D., R.N., and Gina Ogden, Ph.D. *Safe Encounters: How Women Can Say Yes to Pleasure and No to Unsafe Sex.* New York: McGraw-Hill Book Company, 1988.

Wolfe, Linda. *The Cosmo Report.* New York: Arbor House, 1981.

ARTICLES

Abbott-Richmond, Marie, and Nadean Bishop. "The New Old-Fashioned Womanhood." *Human Behavior*, April 1977.

Abrams, Bill. "Why Revlon's Charlie Seems to Be Ready to Settle Down." *The Wall Street Journal*, December 23, 1982.

Ascher, Barbara Lazear. "Hers." *The New York Times*, February 3, 1983.

Bach, George, and Laura Torbet. "Caring In and Out of Bed." *Redbook*, April 1982.

Barron, Deborah Durfee, and Daniel Yankelovich. "Today's American Woman: How the Public Sees Her." Prepared for the President's Advisory Committee for Women by the Public Agenda Foundation. September 1980.

Black, Harvey, and Virginia B. Angelis. "Interpersonal Attraction: An Empirical Investigation of Platonic and Romantic Love." *Psychological Reports*, 34, 3 (June 1974).

Blocki, Linda. "Decoding Manspeak," *Albuquerque Singles Scene*, May 1982.

———. "Fear of Commitment," *Albuquerque Singles Scene*, August 1981.

Bracken, Michael, Lorraine Klerman, and Maryann Bracken. "Coping with Pregnancy Resolution Among Never-Married Women." *American Journal of Orthopsychiatry*, 48, 2 (April 1978).

Bradley, David. "A Man Explains Why I Said 'I'll Call You,' and Didn't." *Savoy*, December 1980.

Brandt, Anthony. "We're Equals, But I'm the Boss." *McCall's*, August 1983.

Callahan, Carol. "How Sex Without Commitment Can Be Good for Your Ego." *Woman*, June 1982.

Cassell, Carol. "Perspective: Male Involvement." In *Emphasis*, published by Education Department, Planned Parenthood Federation, Summer 1981.

"Choosing and Using a Contraceptive." In *Patient Education*, James Bowman Associates, eds. San Francisco: JBA Press, 1977.

Cobliner, W. Godfrey, Harold Schulman, and Vivian Smith. "Patterns of Contraceptive Failures: The Role of Motivation Re-Examined." *Journal of Biosociologic Science*, 7 (1975).

Collins, Glen. "Chemical Connections: Pathways of Love." *The New York Times*, February 14, 1982.

Conway, Jill Ker. "A Proper Perspective." In *Today's Girls, Tomorrow's Women*. New York: Girls Club of America, 1980.

"Dating Rituals." *Human Behavior*, August 1978.

Dion, Kenneth Z., and Karen K. Dion. "Correlates of Romantic Love." *Journal of Consulting Clinical Psychology*, 41, 1 (August 1973).

Donovan, Patricia. "Airing Contraceptive Commercials." NAB survey by *Family Planning Perspectives*, 14, 6 (November-December 1982).

Dretch, James. "Love, Sex Roles and Psychological Health." *Journal of Personality Assessment*, 42, 6 (December 1978).

Dryfoos, Joy G. "Contraceptive Use, Pregnancy Intentions and Pregnancy Outcomes Among U.S. Women." *Family Planning Perspectives*, 2 (March-April 1983).

Dullea, Georgia. "Marriage Versus Living Together." *The New York Times*, February 14, 1983.

Ehrenreich, Barbara. "The Playboy Man and the American Family." *Ms.*, June 1983.

————, Elizabeth Hess, and Gloria Jacobs. "A Report on the Sex Crisis." *Ms.*, March 1982.

Farrell, Warren. "Risking Sexual Rejection: Women's Last Frontier?" *Ms.*, April 1982.

Fengler, Alfred, and Call Middlebury. "Romantic Love in Courtship: Divergent Paths of Male and Female Students." *Journal of Conservative Family Studies*, 4, 17 June, 1974.

Fisher, W. A., D. Byrne, J. Edmunds, C. Miller, K. Kelley, and L. White. "Psychological and Situation-Specific Correlates of Contraception Behavior Among University Women." *Journal of Sex Research*, 15, 1 (1979).

Forrest, Jacqueline, and Richard Fordyce. "U.S. Women's Contraceptive Attitudes and Practice: How Have They Changed in the 1980s?" *Family Planning Perspectives*, 20 (May-June 1988).

Freudenberger, Herbert. "Today's Troubled Men," *Psychology Today*, Volume 21, Number 12, December 1987.

Friedan, Betty. "Feminism's Next Step." *The New York Times*, July 14, 1981.

Geist, William E. "Weddings Flourishing Today." *The New York Times*, May 18, 1982.

Gordon, Sol. "Is Sex Screwing Up Your Relationship?" *Find*, June 1980.

Harvey, S. Marie. "Trends in Contraceptive Use at One University: 1974–1978." *Family Planning Perspectives*, 12 (November-December 1980).

Hellmlich, Nancy. "Marriage Outranks a Career." *U.S.A. Today*, October 5, 1988.

Henshaw, Stanley K., and Jane Silverman. "The Characteristics and Prior Contraceptive Use of U.S. Abortion Patients." *Family Planning Perspectives*, Volume 20, Number 4, July/August 1988.

Herold, Edward S. "Measurement Issues Involved in Examining Contraceptive Use Among Young Single Women." Unpublished paper, Department of Family Studies, University of Guelph, Ontario, Canada, 1980.

————, and Marilyn Shirley Goodwin. "Adamant Virgins, Potential Nonvirgins and Nonvirgins." *Journal of Sex Research*, 17, 2 (May, 1981).

———— and Marilyn Shirley Goodwin. "Premarital Sexual Guilt and Contraceptive Attitudes and Behavior." *Family Relations*, 30 April 1981.

Hoffman, Jan. "Making Up Is Hard to Do." *Village Voice*, May 31, 1983.

Houch, Catherine. "Sex and the American Teen-Ager." *Ladies' Home Journal*, April 1980.

"The Joys of Love." *McCalls*, February 1982.

Kephart, William. "Some Correlates of Romantic Love." *Journal of Marriage and the Family*, 29, 3 (1967).

Korda, Michael. "Sexual Bargaining." *Self*, February 1982.

Korman, Sheila K., and Gerald R. Leslie. "The Relationship of Feminist Ideology and Date Expense Sharing to Perceptions of Sexual Aggression in Dating." *Journal of Sex Research*, 18, 2 (May 1982).

Kumer, Corby. "The Unsinkable Lauren Bacall." *McCall's*, May 1981.

Lederer, Joseph. "Birth Control Decisions." *Psychology Today*, June 1983.

Lee, Madeline. "Oh, Mom, Do We Have to Talk About Sex Again?" *Ms.*, May 1982.

Levin, R. J. "The Redbook Report on Premarital and Extramarital Sex." *Redbook*, October 1975.

Loschiavo, Linda Ann. "5 Traps Single Women Fall into When Looking for Love." *Woman*, March 1988.

Lowry, Pamela. "Unwanted Pregnancy—Why?" Mimeographed paper from Planned Parenthood, 476 West MacArthur Blvd., Oakland, Calif. 94609. Published originally in *Harvard Crimson*, August 10, 1971.

Luker, Kristin. "The Male Role in Family Planning." Conference Proceedings, Office of Family Planning, California Department of Health, June 1977.

Machlowetz, Marilyn. "M.B.A." column, in *Working Women*, March 1982.

Madson, Christine. "Teen Books: Promoting the 'Right' Values?" *Christian Science Monitor*, January 7, 1982.

"Marrying, Divorcing, and Living Together in the U.S. Today." *Population Bulletin*, 32, 5 (February 1979).

Maryless, Daisy, and Robert Dahlin, eds. "Special Report: The World of Romance Fiction." *Publishers Weekly*, 1982.

Miller, Larry. "Man/Woman Desire: Devastating Differences." *Cosmopolitan*, July 1982.

Miller, William B. "Psychological Vulnerability to Unwanted Pregnancy." *Family Planning Perspectives*, 5, 4 (1975).

Morais, Robert, and Allen L. Tan. "Male-Female Differences in Conceptions of Romantic Love Relationships." *Psychological Reports*, 47 (3P-12) (December 1980).

Needle, Richard H. "Factors Affecting Contraceptive Practices of High School and College-Age Students." *Journal of School Health*, 23 (June 1977).

"The New Morality," *Time*, November 21, 1977.

O'Toole, Patricia. "Paperback Virgins." *Human Behavior*, February 1979.

"Planning Status of Marital Births, 1975–1976." *Family Planning Perspectives*, 13, 2 (March/April 1981).

Rader, Gordon E., L. DeMoyne Bekker, Laura Brown, and Cheryl Richardt. "Psychological Correlates of Unwanted Pregnancy." Paper presented at Annual Convention of the American Psychological Association, August 26, 1977.

Reiss, Ira. "Premarital Sexual Standards." *SEICUS* Study Guide No. 5, 1967. Revised, 1975.

"Riding the Romance Range." *Family Circle*, August 11, 1981.

"Right Now," *Glamour*, July 1982.

Rubenstein, Carin. "The Modern Art of Courtly Love." *Psychology Today*, July 1983.

Sanchez, Robert. "Sex—How Sex Appeal Is Used As an Attention Getter." *New Mexico Daily Lobo*, April 2, 1982.

"Sex: Blinking at the Birds and Bees." *Human Behavior*, February 1979.

Siskel, Gene. "America Salutes An Officer and a Gentleman." *Albuquerque Journal*, December 5, 1982.

Snitow, Ann Barr. "Sex in Novels." In *Women: Sex and Sexuality*, Catharine Stimpson and Ethel S. Pearson, eds. University of Chicago Press, 1980.

Solomon, Robert. "Love in the Clique." Psychology Today, October 1982.

Staples, Robert. "The New Sex vs. the Old Ideals." *Essence*, May 1981.

Steinem, Gloria. "The Way We Were—And Will Be." *Ms.*, December 1979.

Sullivan, Barbara. "Shopping for Miss/Mr. Right." *Albuquerque Journal*, July 24, 1988.

Swartz, Jacqueline. "How to Live With—and Love—a Semi-Liberated Man." *New Dawn*, July 1977.

Tepper, Sherri. "So You Don't Want to Be a Sex Object." Denver, Colo.: Rocky Mountain Planned Parenthood, 1973.

Thorton, Arland, and Deborah Freedman. "The Changing American Family." *Population Bulletin*, 38, 4 (October 1983).

Upchurch, Marian L. "Sex Guilt and Contraceptive Use." *Journal of Sex Education and Therapy*, 4, 1 (Spring/Summer 1978).

Walsh, Robert H., and Wilbert M. Leonard. "Usage of Terms for Sexual Intercourse by Men and Women." *Archives of Sexual Behavior*, 3, 4 (1974).

Zelnick, M., and J. F. Kanter. "Sexual and Contraceptive Experience of Young Unmarried Women in the United States, 1976 and 1971." *Family Planning Perspectives*, 9, 2, 1978.

ABOUT THE AUTHOR

Winner of a prestigious Margaret Sanger Award, given to individuals who contributed most to enlightened sexuality in the last decade by The Institute of Family Research and Education, Carol Cassell is a leader in the field of sexuality education. President of The American Association of Sex Educators, Counselors and Therapists, the nation's largest professional organization in this field, Dr. Cassell was also the first director of the Planned Parenthood Federation of America's Department of Education. In that capacity she organized a series of research demonstration projects funded by major national foundations, and consulted with Planned Parenthood's 189 affiliates across the country. She holds a doctorate in community health education and is a member of the Honor Society of Phi Kappa Phi, and is listed in the *Who's Who of American Women*.

Dr. Cassell speaks regularly on topics related to sexuality, including an appearance on a recent Home Box Office special, "Talking to Kids About Sex," currently scheduled for book publication, on NBC's "60 Minutes," and a variety of national and local radio and television shows including "The Phil Donahue Show," "The Today Show", and "Hour Magazine." Her research has been published in such professional journals as the *Journal of Sex Education and Therapy*, on which she serves as a consulting editor, *The Journal of Sex Research* and the *OB/GYN Annual Edition*.

In addition Carol Cassell has received a Certificate of Recognition from Eta Sigma Gamma, the National Professional Health Science Honorary. Dr. Cassell lives in Albuquerque, New Mexico, with her husband. She has four children, and two stepchildren.